Reading Twentieth-Century Poetry

READING TWENTIETH-CENTURY POETRY

POETRY

The Language of Gender and Objects

EDWARD LARRISSY

BASIL BLACKWELL

Copyright © Edward Larrissy 1990
First published 1990

Basil Blackwell Ltd
108 Cowley Road, Oxford, OX4 1JF, UK

Basil Blackwell, Inc.
3 Cambridge Center
Cambridge, Massachusetts 02142, USA

British Library Cataloguing in Publication Data

A CIP catalogue record for this book is available from the British Library.

Library of Congress Cataloging in Publication Data
Larrissy, Edward.
  Reading twentieth century poetry: the language of gender and objects / Edward Larrissy)
    p.   cm.
  Includes bibliographical references.
  ISBN 0–631–15358–6. — ISBN 0–631–15359–4 (pbk.)
  1. American poetry—20th century—History and criticism—Theory, etc.
2. English poetry—20th century—History and criticism—Theory, etc.
3. American poetry—20th century—History and criticism.   4. English poetry—
20th century—History and criticism.   5. Postmodernism (Literature)
6. Romanticism.   I. Title.
PS323.5.L37   1991   90–31564
811'.509—dc20   CIP
Typeset in 11 on 13pt Garamond
by Best-set Typesetter Limited, Hong Kong
Printed in Great Britain by T. J. Press Ltd, Padstow, Cornwall

CONTENTS

ACKNOWLEDGEMENTS

I am indebted to Professor Eric Mottram for inviting me to a colloquium in 1981 on 'The Poetry of Contemporary America' at the University of London Institute of United States Studies, where I conceived the idea of this book partly in response to a paper by Allen Fisher on 'The Referential Discussion' in American Poetry of the 1970s. My subsequent explorations of Pound's work took their bearing from Alan Durant's indispensable book, *Ezra Pound: Indentity in Crisis*, which encouraged me to look at other poets in a similar way.

I am grateful to the editors of the *Yearbook of English Studies* for permitting me to use material that first appeared there in an article on contemporary poetry; and to the editors of *Critical Quarterly* for allowing me the same freedom with material from an article on Ted Hughes, and a review of John Ashbery. And some of the points made in the last chapter were first made in slightly different form at the 'Writing the Future' Conference (1986) of the Warwick University Centre for Research in Philosophy and Literature.

E.L.

The author and publishers wish to thank the following for permission to use copyright material.

Tom Paulin, *Liberty Tree* (1983): "Desert-martin", "Yes, the Maternity Unit", "S/he", "To the Linen Hall": Reprinted by permission of Faber & Faber Ltd from *Liberty Tree* by Tom Paulin.

Ezra Pound, *Collected Shorter Poems*: "Sestina: Altaforte", "Portrait d'une femme", "Hugh Selwyn Mauberley": UK – Reprinted by permission of Faber & Faber from *Collected Shorter Poems* by Ezra Pound. US – Ezra Pound: *Personae*. Copyright © 1926 by Ezra Pound. Reprinted by permission of New Directions Publishing Corporation.

Ezra Pound, *Cantos*: "IV", "LXXXI": UK – Reprinted by permission of Faber & Faber Ltd from *The Cantos of Ezra Pound*. US – Ezra Pound: *The Cantos of Ezra Pound*. Copyright © 1934, 1948 by Ezra Pound. Reprinted by permission of New Directions Publishing Corporation.

Ezra Pound, *Homage to Sextus Propertius*, "I": UK – Reprinted by permission of Faber & Faber from *Collected Shorter Poems* by Ezra Pound. US – Ezra Pound: *Personae*. Copyright © 1926 by Ezra Pound. Reprinted by permission of New Directions Publishing Corporation.

T S Eliot, *Collected Poems*, "The Love Song of J Alfred Prufrock", "Gerontion", "The Waste Land": UK – Reprinted by permission of Faber & Faber Ltd from *Collected Poems 1909–1962* by T S Eliot. US – Excerpts from "The Love Song of J Alfred Prufrock", "Gerontion", and "The Waste Land" from *Collected Poems 1909–1962* by T S Eliot, copyright © 1936 by Harcourt Brace Jovanovich, Inc., copyright © 1964 by T S Eliot, reprinted by permission of the publisher.

William Carlos Williams, *Collected Poems*: "Kora in Hell", "Spring and All", "Poem", "10/22", "The Attick Which is Desire", "Young Woman at a Window", "This is Just to Say", "For Elsie": William Carlos Williams, *Collected Poems Volume I 1909–1939*. Copyright UK – 1938 by Carcanet Press Ltd. © Reprinted by permission of Carcanet Press Ltd. US – William Carlos Williams: *Collected Poems Volume I 1909–1939*. Copyright © 1938 by New Directions Publishing Corporation. Reprinted by permission of New Directions Publishing Corporation.

William Carlos Williams, *Collected Poems*: "Kora in Hell", "Spring and All": US – William Carlos Williams, *Imaginations*. Copyright © 1970 by Florence H Williams. Reprinted by permission of New Directions Publishing Corporation.

Marianne Moore, *Collected Poems*: "The Jerboa", "The Fish": UK – Reprinted by permission of Faber & Faber Ltd from *The Complete Poems of Marianne Moore*. US – Reprinted with permission of Macmillan Publishing Company from *Collected*

Poems by Marianne Moore. Copyright © 1935 by Marianne Moore, renewed 1963 by Marianne Moore and T S Eliot.

Charles Olson, *Selected Writings*: "The Kingfishers": US – Charles Olson: *Selected Writings*. Copyright © 1953 by Charles Olson. Reprinted by permission of New Directions Publishing Corporation.

Charles Olson, *Maximus Poems*: trans / ed by Butterick, George, first published by the University of California Press.

Louis Zukofsky: *A*. Copyright © 1979 by Celia and Louis Zukofsky. Reprinted by permission of the University of California Press.

George Oppen, *Collected Poems*: "Of being numerous", "Image of the engine", "A kind of garden", "Discrete series": Copyright © 1975 by George Oppen. Reprinted by permission of New Directions Publishing Corporation.

Charles Tomlinson, *The Necklace* (1955): "Nine variations in a Chinese winter setting", "Through binoculars": Reprinted by permission of Oxford University Press.

Charles Tomlinson, *Seeing is Believing* (1960): "Geneva restored", "Seeing is believing", "The Atlantic": Reprinted by permission of Oxford University Press.

Charles Tomlinson, *The Way of a World* (1960): "Descartes and the store", "A word in edgeways", "Swimming Chenango Lake", "Adam", "The Chances of Rhyme": Reprinted by permission of Oxford University Press.

Ted Hughes, *The Hawk in the Rain* (1957): "Wind", "Soliloquy", "Macaw and Little Miss", "Song": UK – Reprinted by permission of Faber & Faber Ltd from *The Hawk in the Rain* by Ted Hughes. US – Excerpts from *The Hawk in the Rain* by Ted Hughes. Copyright © 1956, 1957 by Ted Hughes. Reprinted by permission of Harper & Row, Publishers, Inc.

Ted Hughes, *Crow* (1970): "Fragment of an ancient tablet", "Song for a phallus", "Revenge fable": UK – Reprinted by permission of Faber & Faber Ltd from *Crow* by Ted Hughes. US – Excerpts from *Crow* by Ted Hughes. Copyright © 1971 by Ted Hughes. Reprinted by permission of Harper & Row, Publishers, Inc.

Ted Hughes, *Gaudette* (1977): UK – Reprinted by permission of Faber & Faber Ltd from *Gaudette* by Ted Hughes. US – Excerpts from *Gaudette* by Ted Hughes. Copyright © 1977 by Ted Hughes. Reprinted by permission of Harper & Row, Publishers, Inc.

Ted Hughes, *Wodwo* (1960): "Heptonstall": UK – Reprinted by permission of Faber & Faber Ltd from *Wodwo* by Ted Hughes. US – Excerpt from *Wodwo* by Ted Hughes. Copyright © 1960 by Ted Hughes. Reprinted by permission of Harper & Row, Publishers, Inc.

Sylvia Plath, *Collected Poems* (1965): "Cut", "Wuthering Heights", "The Applicant", "Lady Lazarus", "Purdah", "Death & Co", "Ariel", "Fever 103°", "Words", "Kindness": UK – Sylvia Plath: *The Collected Poems*. Copyright © Ted Hughes, 1965 & 1981. Reprinted by permission of Olwyn Hughes. US – From THE COLLECTED POEMS OF SYLVIA PLATH edited by Ted Hughes. Copyright © 1960, 1965, 1971, 1981 by the Estate of Sylvia Plath. Reprinted by permission of Harper & Row, Publishers, Inc.

Seamus Heaney, *Death of a Naturalist* (1966): "Death of a Naturalist", "Digging", "Dawn Shoot": UK – Reprinted by permission of Faber & Faber Ltd from *Death of a Naturalist* by Seamus Heaney. US – Excerpts from "Death of a Naturalist", "Digging" and "Dawn Shoot" from *Poems, 1965–1975* by Seamus Heaney. Copyright © 1966, 1969, 1972, 1975, 1980 by Seamus Heaney. Reprinted by permission of Farrar, Straus and Giroux, Inc.

Seamus Heaney, *North* (1975): "Punishment": UK – Reprinted by permission of Faber & Faber Ltd from *North* by Seamus Heaney. US – Excerpt from "Punishment" from POEMS, 1965–1975 by Seamus Heaney. Copyright © 1966, 1969, 1972, 1975, 1980 by Seamus Heaney. Reprinted by permission of Farrar, Straus and Giroux, Inc.

Seamus Heaney, *Station Island* (1984): "Away from in All", "Sheelagh na gig", "Station Island: XII": UK – Reprinted by permission of Faber & Faber Ltd from *Station Island* by Seamus Heaney. US – Excerpts from "Away From it All", "Sheelagh na Gig" and "Station Island: XII" from STATION ISLAND by Seamus Heaney. Copyright © 1985 by Seamus Heaney. Reprinted by permission of Farrar, Straus and Giroux, Inc.

Craig Raine, *The Onion Memory* (1978): "An Enquiry into two inches of Ivory", "The Grocer", "The Corporation Gardener's Prologue": Reprinted by permission of Oxford University Press.

Craig Raine, *A Martian Sends a Postcard Home* (1979): "A Martian Sends a Postcard Home", "Oberfeldwebel Beckstadt", "Sexual Couplets": Reprinted by permission of Oxford University Press.

Craig Raine, *Rich* (1984): "In Modern Dress", "A Walk in the Country", "Gaugin": Reprinted by permission of Faber & Faber Ltd from *Rich* by Craig Raine.

John Ashbery, *The Tennis Court Oath* (1962): Copyright © 1962 by John Ashbery. Reprinted from *The Tennis Court Oath* by permission of Wesleyan University Press.

John Ashbery, *Self-Portrait in a Convent Mirror* (1975): "Poem in Three Parts", "The One Thing that can Save America", "Grand Galop", "Forties Flick", "Self-Portrait in a Convex Mirror": From *Self-Portrait in a Convent Mirror* by John Ashbery. Copyright © 1972, 1973, 1974, 1975 by John Ashbery.

John Ashbery, *Houseboat Days* (1977): "Daffy Duck in Hollywood": From *Houseboat Days* by John Ashbery. Copyright © 1975, 1976, 1977 by John Ashbery. Reprinted by permission of the publisher, Viking Penguin, a division of Penguin Books USA Inc.

Iain Sinclair, *Lud Heat* (1975): Iain Sinclair, *Lud Heat* (Albion Village Press) 1975. Reprinted by permission of Iain Sinclair.

Ed Dorn, *Slinger* (1975): Ed Dorn, *Slinger* (1975). Reprinted by permission of Duke University Press.

Andrew Motion, *Dangerous Play* "The Whole Truth": Reprinted by permission of the Peters Fraser & Dunlop Group Ltd.

Paul Muldoon, *Why Brownlee Left* (1980): "Immram": UK – Reprinted by permission of Faber & Faber Ltd from *Why Brownlee Left* by Paul Muldoon. US – Reprinted by permission of Wake Forest University Press from *Why Brownlee Left* by Paul Muldoon.

Adrienne Rich, *The Fact of a Doorframe, Poems Selected and New, 1950–1984*: The lines from "The Photograph of the Unmade Bed" are reprinted from THE FACT OF A DOORFRAME, Poems Selected and New, 1950–1984, by Adrienne Rich, by permission of the author and W W Norton & Company, Inc. Copyright © 1984 by Adrienne Rich. Copyright © 1975, 1978 by W W Norton & Company, Inc. Copyright © 1981 by Adrienne Rich.

I

The Inheritance: Romanticism and the Present Day

I

Accurate description has become the touchstone of value for contemporary critics and reviewers of British and Irish poetry, indeed for many poets and readers. It was not always so:

> Behold the place, where if a Poet
> Shin'd in Description, he might show it,
> Tell how the Moon-beam trembling falls
> And tips with silver all the walls...
> But let it (in a word) be said,
> The Moon was up, and Men a-bed.[1]

That it is so now, however, most knowledgeable readers will hardly need strenuous convincing: they will be familiar with the sort of compliments paid to poets by Anthony Thwaite in the latest popular guide, *Poetry Today*, to take but one example. Here Thomas Kinsella is praised for his 'intellectual seriousness', but also for his 'consummate descriptiveness'; Heaney for his 'physical and verbal precision'; Longley for his 'elegant exactness about things seen'; and Craig Raine for what James Fenton calls his release of 'the faculty of perception'.[2] David Trotter, in his highly original book, *The Making of the Reader*, identifies 'comparison' as the method by which the contemporary British poet renders descriptions memorable.[3] He rightly quotes from Ted Hughes's *Poetry in the Making*, so influential in schools and creative writing classes, and indicative of the considered thoughts of Britain's most influential poet. 'It is one of those curious facts,' says Hughes, 'that when two things are compared in a metaphor or a simile, we see both of them much more distinctly than if they were mentioned separately as having nothing to do with each other ... You are forced to look more closely ... How is a dragonfly like a helicopter?'[4] Trotter discerns the same philosophy of comparison at work in *Touchstones*, a series of anthologies edited by Michael and Peter Benton and widely used in secondary schools. He is given to the startling but reasonable conclusion that 'comparison, one of the many different ways in which poems signify, has become a sign for poetry itself: for the entire scope and value of the art,' and he sees in the rise of Craig Raine and other 'Metaphor Men', such as Christopher Reid or David Sweetman, corroboration of this opinion.[5]

But 'comparison' is not the only basis for accuracy, and there are some poets who might claim to be accurate without using it: Charles Tomlinson, perhaps, and certainly Andrew Crozier. Indeed, the obsession with description is only one very large manifestation of a general, but less obvious, conviction: that good writing is, in Craig Raine's memorable phrase, 'the slavey of sense-experience'.[6] Such empiricism is shared by almost all parties, 'establishment' or *soi-disant* 'anti-establishment'. Those who look to Pound ('Language is made out of concrete things') or to Williams ('No ideas but in things') do not disagree fundamentally about terms with those who admire Ted Hughes or even Craig Raine: they tend to disagree about means. And for some writers quite unlike any of these (Kingsley Amis, for instance) empiricism, though it may not demand compulsory description, does exact a mode of writing which presents itself as dependent on nothing but sense-experience or the ideas derived from it.

So prevalent is the empiricist spirit that it readily misrepresents the past: I am no longer surprised when I hear an interpreter refer to the 'concreteness of Donne's poetry', offering the stiff twin compasses as an example. But such an opinion is hardly discouraged by a reading of John Carey's admittedly brilliant book, *John Donne: Life, Mind and Art*, where Ted Hughes is brought in to aid the argument: 'Hughes, like Donne, steps up the physicality of his words till they land on the page like lumps of raw meat'.[7] Professor Carey, who likes his sense-experience rough, is also an important reviewer of new poetry. He called Hughes's language in *Moortown* 'as physical as a bruise' and encouraged the reputation of Craig Raine.[8]

Of course, it is to Eliot's 1921 account of Donne that we owe the 'physical' Donne: an account from which the judicious Professor Carey normally distances himself. And could one not claim that contemporary 'accuracy', 'fidelity', 'description' and 'comparison' are largely an extension of prejudices begotten by Pound and Eliot and nurtured by Leavis? If this is true, as I believe it to be, it is interesting enough. But there are distinctions to be drawn between the first generation of Modernists and the contemporary poets. And the whole of the modern and contemporary period may be illuminated by considering the question how far modern writing has ever escaped from the set of problems that confronted the Romantics: not far, I suspect. This question may seem remote from our period, but I hope to show that, on the contrary, it may help one to understand even the most radical contemporary writing. For we have not yet emerged from the bourgeois epoch consolidated in the revolutions of the Romantic period, and we retain the old problem of the individual, isolated yet aspiring to common meaning, confronting a world from which the deity has absconded or which seems to give, at best, parsimonious evidence of transcendence. To put it another way, the alienation of contemporary society has exacerbated the old Romantic problem of how (or whether) to infuse a world of fascinating but chaotic sense-data with transcendent meaning when one is deprived of agreed myths. The contemporary alienated Metaphor Man is closely allied to the contemporary maker of rickety myths and historical perspectives (Ted Hughes's *Crow*, Geoffrey Hill's *Mercian Hymns*, Seamus Heaney's *North*).[9] This state of affairs is rendered piquant by the continuing tendency of poets in Britain and Ireland to associate Romanticism with all the bad, vague qualities they suppose to be exorcised by their empiricism, which they conceive of as anti-Romantic.

But what of America? There the reign of the thing has never been quite such a simple matter. The influential philosophy of pragmatism was in effect a revision of empiricism which stressed the interestedness of the observer, and accorded validity to the perception of connections between phenomena. These points are picked up by Pound, Williams and Olson in their insistence that the poet is concerned to record relationships between things, and between the observer and things. So greatly does this complicate matters, in fact, that it is right to see Williams as an important influence on the form taken by the confessional poetry of Robert Lowell, for Williams's directness was not embarrassed by the use of emotive statement unsupported by symbolic objects; and Lowell acknowledged his influence on *Life Studies*.

II

Few scholars and critics of Romanticism are today prepared even to waste time scoffing at the early Modernist estimate of Romantic poetry which tended to find it marked by vagueness, egotism and emotive excess.[10] Indeed, although there are recognized differences among the Romantics, the period as a whole shows an unprecedented empirical bent. This is scarcely surprising, since many Romantic preoccupations and methods arose out of the empiricist philosophies of the Enlightenment. The paintings of Constable and Turner provide analogies. Victorian and modern poets have refined and extended this bent, but they have not relinquished it.

Emotive language is a characteristic the modern period can honestly say it has tried to avoid. Indeed, the 'spirit of anti-pathos', as David Trotter calls it, is pervasive in the twentieth century.[11] It is also conceived, more or less clearly, as anti-Romantic. In certain writers it might better be called the spirit of anti-passion. Nevertheless, this spirit itself derives from the Romantic desire to separate authentic from inauthentic emotion, most clearly and uncompromisingly seen in *Lyrical Ballads*. But it has to be said that the modern aversion to stated emotion, combined with the common dislike of rhetoric, is a fairly distinctive feature of our period. The irony is that, by virtue of this feature, modern poetry distinguishes itself not only from the Romantics and Victorians but from all previous periods as well. Yet Romanticism remains the parent modern writers in Britain are most anxious to disavow, whether they be 'Modernists' or not.

Not that all modern writers have been able to conceal their indebtedness. Edward Lobb, in *T. S. Eliot and the Romantic Critical Tradition*, shows not only that 'Eliot's more extreme criticisms [of the Romantics] in themselves suggest the existence of a kinship which Eliot seeks to deny';[12] but also that such a kinship does indeed exist, particularly with the critical ideas of Keats and Coleridge. But contemporary poets and reviewers in Britain still take their cue from remarks like those of F. R. Leavis in *Revaluation* on Shelley's 'weak grasp upon the actual'. According to Kingsley Amis, in 'Against Romanticism', that degenerated style emerges when writers grow tired of the 'temperate zone' (presumably Classicism) and begin to 'please an ingrown taste for anarchy'. There is also a sneering reference to the supposed Romantic taste for the 'abstract noun'.[13] To the empiricist the abstract noun may suggest a 'weak grasp upon the actual'. Blake Morrison has rightly referred to the popularity in the 1950s of logical positivism and of A. J. Ayer's *Language, Truth and Logic*, first published in 1936 and reissued in 1946: Ayer maintains that 'no statement which refers to a reality transcending the limits of all possible sense-experience can possibly have any literal significance.'[14] To poets untrained in philosophy such statements might even seem to render suspect the abstract noun.

Of course, it is well known that Amis and the other Movement poets were reacting, to a greater or lesser degree, against a brief interregnum of 'neo-Romanticism' in the 1940s, epitomized for them by the personality, as much as by the poetry, of Dylan Thomas. And our own contemporaries may fancy they have another kind of 'Romanticism' to react against: confessional poetry. As A. Alvarez says in his introduction to *The New Poetry: An Anthology*, Robert Lowell and John Berryman were 'no longer concerned with Eliot's rearguard action against the Late Romantics; they were, I mean, no longer adherents of the cult of rigid impersonality.'[15] But in the introduction to the new *Penguin Book of Contemporary British Poetry*, Blake Morrison and Andrew Motion reject the example of Alvarez's anthology. They state that the idea of a link between 'gravity of object and quality of achievement' is regarded with 'scorn' by 'many young writers', and that the example of Heaney has replaced that of Lowell and Berryman. The change represented by Heaney's advancement, it is claimed, is one from language as 'instrument' to language as object: 'Alvarez praised Lowell, Hughes, et al. for dealing with their experience "nakedly", and he presented language as a mere instrument in a therapeutic transaction between writer and reader. Heaney is characteristically more oblique; and he delights in language, relishing it . . . as something that embodies politics, history and locality, as well as having its own delectability.'[16]

There are several things to observe about this: first, whatever Alvarez thinks, it is clear that none of his prized poets (Lowell, Berryman, Hughes or Plath) in fact uses language without a very high degree of artifice; secondly, Motion and Morrison, in attempting to depict Heaney as a lover of language's autonomy, immediately concede that for him it 'embodies politics, history and locality'; thirdly, the symbolic opposition of generations is deeply misleading (though one can understand the editors' desire to set themselves apart from their influential predecessor). For the descent of the Metaphor Man can be traced back to Plath and Hughes, and Heaney is profoundly influenced by Hughes and, to a lesser extent, by Lowell. Where Motion and Morrison really dissent from Alvarez is in the matter of 'personality' and 'extremity'. But here they have been misled by Alvarez's procedure, which always seemed perverse and tendentious, of lumping Plath, Berryman and Lowell together with the British. There has been no earthquake in British poetry. If Ian Hamilton (included by Alvarez) seems a little like Lowell, he is nevertheless more chaste, barbered, suavely reticent: a British Lowell. Andrew Motion himself would not disown these poems. Indeed, it may be worth noting that Motion's name was first widely heard in the mid-1970s in an atmosphere where Hamilton was still regarded as a rising star, and that Motion's poem 'Inland' (which won the Newdigate Prize at Oxford in 1975) was first published in Hamilton's *The New Review* early in 1976.[17]

No: British poetry is doggedly faithful, even in the face of its own contrary practice, to the ideal of a refurbished neo-Classicism, to empiricism, and to anti-Romantic prejudice. The last poem in Tom Paulin's *Liberty Tree* is surprisingly like a contemporary reworking of Amis's 'Against Romanticism'.

> After extremity
> art turns social
> and it's more than fashion
> to voice the word we.

The epic yawp
hangs like an echo
of the big bang,
though now we tell children
to shun that original – . . .
There is a ban
on philosophies of blood,
a terse demand
for arts and skills
to be understood.

('To the Linen Hall')[18]

Paulin has, until recently, been faithful to that 'empiricist attitude' (as I shall call it) which characterized the Movement poets. This attitude, sceptical, discursive, rationalist with a small 'r', can be contrasted with the poetry of what I shall call the 'empiricist moment', which cultivates the vivid rendering of moments of perception. Even in *Liberty Tree* the 'empiricist attitude' can still be seen, as in that fine epitome of Ulster Protestantism, 'Desert-martin':

A Jock squaddy glances down the street
And grins, happy and expendable,
Like a brass cartridge. He is a useful thing,
Almost at home, and yet not quite, not quite.

. . . I see a plain
Presbyterian grace sour, then harden,
As a free strenuous spirit changes
To a servile defiance that whines and shrieks
For the bondage of the letter.

This blend of observation and verified generalization is perfectly acceptable to the 'empiricist attitude'. It could almost be a Movement poem. But it consorts with others that employ different methods. The urbane discursiveness is troubled by a taste for the *mot juste* that surprises, whether exotic ('In the bistre bistro . . .') or, more usually, Scots-Ulster ('your man Craig / keeks at his briar'). This taste goes well with a new foregrounding of the exact but unexpected epithet. Consider this, about a newborn baby:

> Behind sealed windows
> each tiny grub must yell
> inside a plastic cell,
> be topped and tailed
> before its feed
> and with a goldfish mouth
> gnaw the embossed nibble
> on a tender shield,
> until, heavy-headed,
> a clubbed frown,
> it contemplates the wind
> and blurps a verdict.
>
> (From 'Yes, the Maternity Unit')

Much of this is poetry of the empiricist moment: of the vivid capturing of things seen. Paulin's version differs very little from that of the Metaphor Men. He dwells less gloatingly on the metaphors implicit in each of his unexpected epithets. It is more a matter of renewing individual words: a neo-Classicist's Martianism.

Dialect words ('I'd be dead chuffed if I could catch/the dialects of those sea-loughs,' remarks Paulin in 'Politik') are a sub-category of the same concern: an enlargement of the vocabulary of urbane diction, but sanctioned by the dictionary, and all in the service of exactness. In so far as this is a linguistic exoticism, as it clearly is for most of Paulin's readers, it is still safely a matter of precision with individual nouns, verbs and adjectives (usually with a fairly concrete meaning). It is far more acceptable than the kind of exoticism that involves rhetoric or 'abstract nouns': that of John Ashbery, for instance, whose poetry, says Paulin, is 'littered with clichés and lumps of junk diction'.[19] It never occurs to him that all of Ashbery's poems operate within invisible quotation marks, and cannot be seen in terms of the empiricist's idea of language as a nicely wiped window on the world. They are, rather, pieces of studied interpretation which make knowing use of cliché and banality.

In the same place Paulin is also much concerned to suggest, against Helen Vendler, that Ashbery's diction is not 'American': 'His style is not oral, nor is it American.' 'Americanness' is important because, although it might seem to possess dubious status as an aesthetic term, it is the guarantor of authenticity. For Ashbery is American, therefore his style must be American. If his style is not American, his poems are not sincere and his language is not 'rooted' (which is also why his poems are not 'oral'). Therefore the poems are bad: QED. Paulin's stance is un-reflectively left-Leavisite, empiricist and organicist: it demands 'the very language of men'.

Paulin's dialect words enable him to evade the censure he imposes on Ashbery. His own language is 'rooted', albeit, like Wordsworth's, some-what artificially. It also provides him with a not particularly subtle liaison with that popular personage, History. This scarcely strenuous relationship can endear him to his left-liberal readership. The place where leftist sympathy joins with the native empiricism is a very British location: far more British than it is Irish, and more empiricist than it is Marxist. It is a place where people genuflect to the folk and its gritty usages: the left wing of those who like being 'bruised' by Ted Hughes.

An interest in History accounts for another new method of Paulin's: the association between Northern Ireland and other countries with colo-nial or revolutionary associations. Consider the end of 'S/he', where the narrator returns from a visit to the theatre in Derry:

> It stuck close to me, though,
> how all through the last half
> a helicopter held itself
> above the Guildhall –
> Vershinin's lines were slewed
> by the blind chopping blades,
> though Olga looked chuffed
> when she sighed, 'Won't it be odd
> with no soldiers on the streets?'

The connection suggests that there is a similarity between the tense, expectant, pre-revolutionary mood of *The Three Sisters* and the mood of contemporary Northern Ireland. It also provides a striking example of the intrusiveness of the Troubles. History permits such imaginative effects, for it guarantees their basis in objectivity. History is the empiri-cist's imaginativeness, it would seem. The very fine 'Book of Juniper' is as radical as anything Paulin has done, providing fragments linked by the symbol of juniper rather than by an implied historical analysis. But there is not as much of this inventiveness in individual poems as his publishers would like to suggest ('the dazzling juxtapositions and the shifting sense of time and space' (dust jacket)).

Such moments of historical vision probably correspond to what Paulin calls 'vision' in his *Thomas Hardy: The Poetry of Perception*. He himself says, in this curiously inconclusive book, that 'much of what I've said has been an attempt to show how firmly [Hardy's] work is tied to positivism and sceptical empiricism.' Yet he claims to value most those moments when Hardy 'breaks out of Hume's imaginative universe and achieves a visionary freedom'.[20] Thus, in his discussion of 'During Wind and Rain', Paulin refers vaguely to 'images packed with facts that have been transformed by the imagination'.[21] But all that Hardy has done is to transcend Paulin's tendentiously narrow definition of empiricism. For the empiricist is not expected to renounce imagination, merely to base it on facts, as Paulin here praises Hardy for doing. Shelley, Hardy's idol, and another lover of Hume, could be said to write about 'facts transformed by the imagination'. Yet Paulin, in a remark that does him some discredit, airily pronounces that 'Shelley's Romanticism has been largely discredited nowadays.'[22]

III

Perhaps the most trenchant expression of the view that sees Romanticism as unprecedentedly 'objective' is to be found in Geoffrey Thurley's combative book, *The Romantic Predicament*, in which he goes so far as to refer to the 'Rise of Object-Dominance' in the Romantic period:

> From this time onwards, things – phenomena, objects – begin to exist in their own right and for their own sake. The poet's concern is still with meaning, we note, not with natural history. But in order to gain meaning – to be poetic – the poet now requires the thing to be itself, not the emblem of some anterior world-view, and this . . . marks off his work from that of earlier poets.[23]

And this is what later poets of every persuasion share with the Romantics. Not that Thurley ignores our old friend Romantic subjectivity:

'Romantic subjectivism is to be explained as a shift in contents, by which certain ranges of feeling and perception themselves became objective: subjectivity – the mind's processes and movements – itself becomes objective.'[24] Thurley puts well the new status of the object. And his suggestion that subjectivity becomes part of the 'objective' is true for certain types of poem, at least as regarded from certain aspects: Coleridge's 'Conversation Poems', for instance. Of course, Thurley's argument is contentious, at least in the sense that it may not seem to do full justice to the idealist current in Romanticism. Isobel Armstrong, in *Language as Living Form in Nineteenth Century Poetry*, argues that Romantic poetry expresses a philosophical idealism in its very language.[25] For her, Hopkins is the forerunner of Modernism: the first poet to defer to the real otherness of the object, a poet repelled by the Romantics' assimilation of the processes of nature to the processes of mind, and by their insistence on the creative primacy of the mind. Hopkins is held to be trying to transcribe the otherness, the independent reality, of the world, in his use of language.

But what sort of Romantic idealism are we talking about? It is not clear whether Armstrong would agree with Frank Lentricchia, who, in *The Gaiety of Language*, sees Romantic poetry, and in particular the theory and practice of Coleridge, as far more deeply indebted to Friedrich Schelling's *Naturphilosophie* than to Kant's more profoundly transcendental idealism.[26] For Kant, in *The Critique of Pure Reason*, experience from the senses was only ordered into knowledge by the understanding (*Verstand*), which imposed its forms on the content of experience. Coleridge was attracted by Kant's view, and by the contrast with the passivity of mind envisaged in the empiricist tradition of Locke and Hume and Hartley, to which he himself had originally been loyal. But Kant also believed that the essences of things were unknowable: the 'thing in itself' was precisely that, and it remained beyond the grasp of human understanding. Coleridge found this idea hard to swallow:

> In spite therefore of [Kant's] own declarations, I could never believe, that it was possible for him to have meant no more by his *Noumenon*, or THING IN ITSELF, than his mere words express; or that in his whole conception he confined the whole *plastic* power to the forms of the intellect, leaving for the external cause, for the *materiale* of our sensations, a matter without form, which is doubtless inconceivable.[27]

Coleridge was drawn to Schelling's *System of Transcendental Idealism* because, as Lentricchia says, 'Schelling insisted that knowledge itself could not be possible unless there was a fusion of subject and object.'[28] For Schelling there is a continuity, or 'pre-established harmony', between the objective world and the mind. And this continuity is based on the interdependence of spirit and the world of nature. As Coleridge puts it:

> Whatever in its origin is objective, is likewise as such necessarily finite. Therefore, since the spirit is not originally an object, and as the subject exists in antithesis to an object, the spirit cannot originally be finite. But neither can it be a subject without becoming an object, and, as it is originally the identity of both, it can be conceived neither as infinite nor finite exclusively, but as the most original union of both. In the existence, in the reconciling, and the recurrence of this contradiction consists the process and mystery of production and life.[29]

Yet to give the impression of an easy merging of mind and matter (such as might be encouraged by Lentricchia) would be quite unfair to Coleridge, and to Schelling. The striking thing about Schelling's descriptions of nature is the extent to which they make it appear hard to understand and assimilate. The successful recuperation of nature to the structures of the mind is a labour, a quest:

> Everywhere nature first confronts us in more or less hard form and closed in. It is like that serious and silent beauty which does not attract attention by clamorous signs, does not catch the common eye. How can we, so to speak, spiritually melt this apparently hard form, so that the unadulterated energy of things fuses with the energy of our spirits, forming a single cast? We must go beyond form, in order to regain it as comprehensible, and truly felt.[30]

And, perhaps more strikingly,

> What we call nature is a poem that lies hidden in a mysterious and marvellous script. Yet if the riddle could reveal itself, we would recognize in it the Odyssey of the spirit which, in a strange delusion, seeking itself, flees itself; for the land of phantasy [Phantasie] toward which we aspire

gleams through the world of sense only as through a half-transparent
mist, only as a meaning does through words.[31]

As far as immediate experience is concerned, nature remains mysterious,
a riddle to be solved. So even if Schelling's views are taken to run
parallel with Coleridge's poetic thoughts, the poems would not necessarily seem more akin to Schelling than to Kant. For both writers might
be used to support the idea of the mysteriousness of nature. In any case,
is it not characteristic of poems that they leave it unclear what philosophical positions might be deduced from them? What, for instance,
are the full and exact metaphysical implications of these lines from
Coleridge's 'Dejection: An Ode'?

> O Lady! we receive but what we give,
> And in our life alone does Nature live:
> Ours is her wedding garment, ours her shroud!
> And would we aught behold, of higher worth,
> Than that inanimate cold world allowed
> To the poor loveless ever-anxious crowd,
> Ah! from the soul itself must issue forth
> A light, a glory, a fair luminous cloud
> Enveloping the Earth —
> And from the soul itself must there be sent
> A sweet and potent voice of its own birth,
> Of all sweet sounds the life and element!

Does this imply a Kantian imposition of form on the material of
sensation, with the thing in itself hovering unknowably in the background? Or is it more akin to Schelling's 'hard' nature? Scholarship says
that Kant must be the 'influence' here. But we have seen that Coleridge
was dissatisfied with Kant. And as far as his critical writings are
concerned, as Paul Hamilton says, 'If Coleridge were solely a Kantian or
exclusively a follower of Schelling, then things would be much simpler
for his commentators. In fact he displays both influences.'[32] Better to say
that many Romantic poems stress the creative powers of the poet in
ordering the materials of experience. And there are many that place an
equally strong emphasis on the poet's inability to muster these creative
powers. At the level of technique there is much that does not seek a

representational mode of writing, much that overwhelms the conception of a world of objects with the poet's attitudes. But equally there is much that strives to paint that world according to the unprecedented empirical bent to which I have referred.

A Coleridge poem most unlike 'Dejection', such as 'This Lime-Tree Bower my Prison' (1797) strives to mimic the spontaneous movement of the mind, largely in its response to nature. That movement, as in the other 'Conversation Poems', is dialectical: we start with Coleridge, disabled by an accident, sitting disconsolately in his bower and thinking of his friends, who have been able to go on a walk. He pictures the experiences they will have. In the second verse-paragraph he imagines that they will experience the presence of 'the Almighty Spirit' beneath the veils of Nature, in this case in the sight of a sunset, as he has done in the past. In the third and final verse-paragraph Coleridge, moved by a delighted moment of Romantic sympathy with the imagined pleasures of his friends, is able himself to find intense pleasure in the details of the scene around him in his lime-tree bower. He even blesses the rook (traditionally ill-omened) and thinks of his friend Charles Lamb as charmed by its 'creaking' because for him (as for Coleridge) 'No sound is dissonant which tells of Life.' This is the concluding line of the poem. And it also symbolizes the idea that Coleridge's condition, and his complaint about it, have redeemed themselves from evil associations by 'telling of life'. And the poem does not merely tell in the sense of discoursing: its movement (from confinement, to imagined encounter with the Almighty Spirit, to redeemed confinement) is meant to exhibit the spontaneous dialectical workings of the mind, and to suggest that these workings are those of Life in general. Coleridge tended to see the dynamic tension of opposite states or principles, producing a third term from their interaction, as essential to the structure of the universe. Before he had studied the German philosophers he was already disposed, by his reading in the mystics, especially perhaps Jakob Boehme, to think in this way. Scientific discoveries, such as the positive and negative poles of electricity, seemed to confirm this predisposition (though in the case of electricity he lamented the lack of a third term to synthesize the other two.) Thus, in a poem such as 'This Lime-Tree Bower', it is not surprising to see a reflection of the Christian pattern of Eden–Fall–Redemption superimposed on a movement analagous to the systolic rhythm of the heart.[33] Of a poem like this it may be a slightly misleading half-truth to say, as Isobel Armstrong does, that 'For Romantic language analogies are made in and through the process of perception and the creation of categories'.[34] For although this is the way the poem works, it only does so because Coleridge believes that the analogies really do exist in Nature as a whole.

But however consoling it may have been to believe it, the very structure of the 'Conversation Poems' suggests a certain difficulty in reaching this belief in the face of the immediate experience of things: the consoling and harmonized endings can only be arrived at after a Fall. Nature, though delightfully, 'affronts us in more or less hard form and closed in', for Coleridge was ready for Schelling even before he had read him.

It is partly for this reason that the delightful detailed descriptions to be found in many Coleridge poems offer their riches far in excess of the requirements of any thesis. Thus, in the first part of 'This Lime-Tree Bower' we find the detailed description of the 'roaring dell', into which we are asked to imagine his friends descending:

> The roaring dell, o'erwooded, narrow, deep,
> And only speckled by the mid-day sun;
> Where its slim trunk the ash from rock to rock
> Flings arching like a bridge; – that branchless ash,
> Unsunn'd and damp, whose few poor yellow leaves
> Ne'er tremble in the gale, yet tremble still,
> Fann'd by the water-fall! and there my friends
> Behold the dark green file of long lank weeds,
> That all at once (a most fantastic sight!)
> Still nod and drip beneath the dripping edge
> Of the blue clay-stone.

The point about this is not that it looks strange to us moderns: it does not. We understand very well a poem that devotes many of its energies to description. Not that this passage lacks symbolic intent. For the descent into the dell to find pleasure even there mirrors the total pattern of redemptive descent. The point is that the descriptions are not neatly folded into this purpose: they go beyond it, offering themselves simply as the pleasure of the senses. We understand this offering so well. It is

Coleridge's rounded, philosophical argument that appears slightly out-moded. To poets before the middle of the eighteenth century, however, the energy invested in procuring the sense of fidelity for such descrip-tions, the amount of space given to them and the redundance in them, would have seemed outlandish. Nature has become a problem to be described in accurate detail, not a storehouse of conventional imagery. And Coleridge hopes that he can show that the answer to the problem is that you end up by perceiving the 'Almighty Spirit'.

Another by-product of empiricism is present in Coleridge: the attempt to register accurately the movement of the mind. The sinuous movement of the verse, the conversational style, the present tense, the exclamatory tone – all are enlisted in this attempt, of which the chief engine is Association of Ideas. This is an essential component of em-piricist psychology, and one familiar to all students of Wordsworth and Coleridge. Its workings can be seen most clearly in Coleridge's 'Frost at Midnight'. Here Coleridge sits by the side of his sleeping baby son, otherwise alone, envisaging the quiet growth of frost in the night outside. He hears the fluttering of a film of soot (called a 'stranger') on the grate. Association of ideas takes his mind back to his schooldays in the city when he would be lulled to sleep contemplating the same type of film and dreaming of his country home. The next day he would be unable to concentrate on his book, though under the eye of the 'stern preceptor'. But he would be hoping to see the face of a 'stranger' – someone unknown to the school, who had come up from his country home to see him: relatives, or perhaps his sister who played with him when they were both infants. The thought of infancy propels his mind back to the sleeping baby beside him, and he begins to reflect that this child will be educated by Nature, not merely by the book. Thus it will come to appreciate all seasons, and all aspects of the seasons, including a frosty night. Coleridge perceptively finds a pattern in association: the ideas cluster around the concept of education. And the poem strives to depict the connectedness of different levels of the mind: intellection, private feelings, verbal play.

That may serve to remind us that associationism is the ancestor of 'Dissociation of Sensibility'. This can readily be seen from the writings of Rémy de Gourmont, who influenced Eliot's formulation of the dis-sociation theory. It is interesting to look at de Gourmont's essay, 'The

Dissociation of Ideas', from two angles: that of Romanticism and that of Eliot. The Romantic – empiricist provenance of some modern prejudices is immediately cast into exceptionally clear relief: 'There are no ideas so remote, no images so incongruous, that an easy freedom of association cannot join them at least for the moment . . . even while we perceive no less well their delicious absurdity.'[35] The first part of these remarks would be no surprise to Coleridge. The latter part, about delicious absurdity, points chiefly to the more modern use of association. It is true, of course, that Coleridge's association of ideas in the poems we have looked at is not free in an absolute sense. The dialectical movement of association is seen as a basic feature of the mind, and one which mirrors that dynamic tension of opposites he would like to see as fundamental to the structure of the universe. But the point is that moderns have extracted from the broad inheritance of Wordsworth and Coleridge what they feel they can still believe in: namely, the possible (but possibly impossible) significance of objects; and the tracing of the mind's movement 'on the spot'. And although objects are folded, by Wordsworth and Coleridge, into an idealistic scheme, they remain recalcitrant to this folding by virtue of a certain stubbornness and redundance of detail.

The belief in the conformity of mind and objects leads to the conception of the poem as living letter, for words ideally partake both of the mind and of things: 'Words are the living products of the living mind and could not be a due medium between the thing and the mind unless they partook of both.'[36] It is because they partake of the life of the mind that words are 'living things',[37] and, 'any harmony in the things symbolized will perforce be presented to us more easily as well as with additional beauty by a correspondent harmony of the Symbols with each other.'[38] To evince the harmony in the things symbolized is the same as to affirm the harmony of mind and objects, which is the same as to create a harmony between words. For this reason language is properly seen, for Coleridge, in those terms of von Humboldt with which he would have agreed: 'Language is not a work (*ergon*) but an activity (*energeia*).'[39] But it depends on the poet to mobilize this activity. For words may rest inert and arbitrary. Coleridge asks, 'Is *thinking* impossible without arbitrary signs? &–how far is the word "arbitrary" a misnomer?'[40] Because 'the Word is the first Birth of the Idea, and it's flexible organ' the relation between signifier and signified is indissoluble, and in that sense non-arbitrary, for Coleridge.[41] Yet he does not believe in some indicative relationship between them. The poet has to recover the vulnerable vitality of words through the relationship of discourse and world and thus restore an Adamic or quasi-divine language. But since the poem moves from dejected or unimaginative consciousness to renewed perception, it shows that such a language has to be worked for. And this movement reveals a division in the self: 'the relatively self-conscious self and that self within the self', as Geoffrey Hartman puts it.[42] Or, rather than the self within the self, say the self that is wider than the ego, the self that is identified with the infinity of desire and the infinity of Imagination, echoes of the infinity of Nature and God. The world of Nature has the task, in Wordsworth and Coleridge, of evincing the divinity of things. Yet this divinity remains, as far as the poem is concerned, a *fiat* of consciousness. The fact that Coleridge is moved to ecstatic apostrophe by the setting sun and the clouds, or that he takes delight in the lime-tree bower itself, may prove that he feels a love of Nature. And the fact that he is able to imagine the pleasure of his absent friends may prove his capacity for 'sympathy'. But the evident sub-text about the reconciliation of contraries as a fundamental structure of things, maintained by the Almighty Spirit, is not proved by anything except his own faith in it. One is left with a large residue of relatively pure description: the irreducibly 'hard' world of Nature. And yet without that world there would be no poem.

One may posit, then, a triad in Coleridge's poems: self-conscious self; world of natural objects; renewed self. What the self-conscious self takes from the world of natural objects is a sense of its own enlargement through sympathy or sublimity. But the poem does not prove that natural objects effect this, only that the poet believes, or wishes to believe, that this is true. Natural objects are the perceptible veil of what is desired to be there: 'of such hues / As veil the Almighty Spirit, when yet he makes / Spirits perceive his presence.' They thus have to perform the function of filling the split in the self, while at the same time their inability to do so convincingly reveals both the ineradicability of that split, and the strength of the self-generated wish to overcome it through the Other of Nature. But this Other only serves as an objective reminder of the self's alienation.

This difficult relationship of self and natural objects accounts for the ease with which commentators may describe one or the other of Wordsworth and Coleridge as either too egotistical or, on the other hand, markedly objective. Thus Hazlitt on Wordsworth: 'an intense intellectual egotism swallows up every thing', while Coleridge allows natural objects their autonomy.[43] Coleridge himself, like Keats, was capable of thinking about Wordsworth in the same way. Yet he also impugns him for 'matter-of-factness'. And it has often been noted that Coleridge himself has a tendency to swallow things up in intellectual egotism. For many modern critics it is Wordsworth who is the founder of the line of objectivity. Thus David Moody says that, 'throughout his best work there is a consistent critique of the habit of preferring our own associations to the object in itself.'[44] And it is possible for the structuralist Michael Riffaterre to conclude a complex and sensitive analysis of Wordsworth's 'Yew Trees', with its peaceful sound of murmuring waters, in this manner.

> The poem begins with meditation and foresight to end with the mere recording of present experience. Far from being a letdown after the symbolic meanings of the first part, the strict literalness of the end is a climax. Its significance lies in the meaninglessness of the sound. Sensation is all – which is exactly what descriptive poetry is about.[45]

But though a tendency of our argument has been that it may be understandable to *think* that sensation is all in some Wordsworth poems, sensation is not all. Earlier in the poem we have had

> This solitary Tree! a living thing
> Produced too slowly ever to decay;
> Of form and aspect too magnificent
> To be destroyed.

This solitary tree can be compared to 'The immeasurable height/Of woods decaying, never to be decayed' (*Prelude*, VI (1805), 556–7), Wordsworthian emblem of the endurance of the natural cycle. The yew tree is also an emblem of a quiet, receptive mode of being, open to natural influences, suggesting this mode to the speaker, who is thus receptive to the sound of the waters. This sound is itself a repeated Wordsworthian theme, either as lulling, or else, more ambiguously, as in

> The torrents shooting from the clear blue sky,
> The rocks that muttered close upon our ears,
> Black drizzling crags that spake by the wayside
> As if a voice were in them.
>
> *(Prelude*, VI (1805), 561–64)

In this passage ('Crossing the Alps') Nature's recovered status as divine book and the poem's achieved status as living letter become most obvious. Straying from the correct path, the path of stereotyped tourist expectation and response, which might have led to a conventionally sublime poem, the travellers cross the Alps without knowing it, only to be told that they have already done so: *'That we had crossed the Alps'*. The words are italicized in the 1850 version, stressing the phrase as phrase. And indeed it does have a powerful impact on the speaker, who is halted and thrown into a nearly trance-like state in which he apostrophizes Imagination. The words, in their flatness, are like a parody and reduction of the conventional descripition. But by virtue of that very inadequacy they propel the speaker into a powerful sense of the true awesomeness of the experience he might have had.

The Prelude contains several such patent questionings of the adequacy of the letter and its tendency to produce an inadequate description of experience. The passage on the blind London beggar sees Wordsworth straying 'out of the reach of common indication'. Thus, already freed from the fixity of conventional signification, he encounters the beggar,

> Wearing a written paper to explain
> The story of the man, and who he was.
> My mind did at this spectacle turn round
> As with the might of waters, and it seemed
> To me that in this label was a type,
> Or emblem, of the utmost that we know,
> Both of ourselves and of the universe;
> And, on the shape of the unmoving man,
> His fixèd face and sightless eyes, I looked,
> As if admonished from another world.
>
> (VII (1805), 613–22)

Again, the label points to a state of affairs much larger than it can indicate: it acts as a metonym, denoting a part but connoting a whole.

And in Book XI (1805), having lost his way, the youthful Wordsworth encounters the mouldered remains of a gibbet-mast, under which the letters of the murderer's name are cut into the turf, 'by superstition of the neighbourhood' kept 'fresh and visible' (297, 299). It is the sight of these 'characters', rather than anything else in the place, that causes Wordsworth to flee: 'forthwith I left the spot' (302). When he does so he comes upon a beacon and a girl carrying a pitcher on her head. Although this is 'An ordinary sight', nevertheless Wordsworth says he would need 'Colours and words that are unknown to man / To paint the visionary dreariness' which invested the scene at this moment (309 – 11). Yet again there is a movement from inadequate letters to the awful sense of what they cannot contain. This sense is then displaced onto the 'ordinary sight', which becomes matter for an impossible task of restoration through 'colours' and, significantly enough, 'words'.

   To return to the crossing of the Alps. The poet's imagination, set free by the destruction of the possibility of stock response, reacts to the scene with a sensitivity supposedly free, and adequate: a considerable accomplishment. The travellers' road enters a narrow chasm, where the poet can see

> The immeasurable height
> Of woods decaying, never to be decayed,
> The stationary blasts of waterfalls,
> And everywhere along the hollow rent
> Winds thwarting winds, bewildered and forlorn,
> The torrents shooting from the clear blue sky,
> The rocks that muttered close upon our ears,
> Black drizzling crags that spake by the wayside,
> As if a voice were in them, the sick sight
> And giddy prospect of the raving stream
> The unfettered clouds and region of the Heavens,
> Tumult and peace, the darkness and the light –
> Were all like workings of one mind, the features
> Of the same face, blossoms upon one tree;
> Characters of the great Apocalypse,
> The types and symbols of Eternity,
> Of first, and last, and midst, and without end.

(556 – 72)

The sense of the poet's being 'unfettered' is inscribed in the passage itself. But the word also helps to suggest the difficulty of fitting the scene into any description, let alone a stereotyped one. There is something incoherent and chaotic about the elements of the scene themselves, as well as the whole. The whole is intended to present a harmonious reconciliation of contraries ('tumult and peace, the darkness and the light') prefigured in the 'immeasurable height / Of woods decaying, never to be decayed, / The stationary blasts of waterfalls'. Yet the sense of contraries embraces contrariety ('Winds thwarting winds, bewildered and forlorn') and even a slightly terrifying anarchy: the accent is on 'tumult' rather than 'peace'. But having presented contraries as reconciled, Wordsworth goes on to see them as the features of 'one mind' and as the living letters of a Holy Book of Nature, restored with difficulty – difficulty he smooths over.

In an illuminating essay, 'The Eye and Progress of his Song: a Lacanian Reading of *The Prelude*', Robert Young attempts to elucidate the role of natural objects, and the split in the self, in terms of the theories of Jacques Lacan. In particular he draws on the concepts of the *objet petit a*, and the *Spaltung*, or split. But to explain these terms needs some rehearsal of Lacan's ideas about the 'mirror phase', about the formation of the human subject in language, and about its emergence, from a purely Imaginary relation with an other, into the Symbolic.

He sees the infant after birth as lacking any sense of coherence, let alone identity. The infant is *l'hommelette* (little man and omelette: shattered egg). In the mirror phase, which occurs around six months, the child recognizes itself in the mirror. This occurrence is symbolic of an event which would occur whether or not there were an actual mirror: 'the symbolic matrix in which the *I* is precipitated in a primordial form'.[46] In fact the infant is deriving its sense of its own identity from an identification with the mother: 'the specular image ... serve[s] as a homologue for the Mother / Child symbolic relation.'[47] The illusory sense of wholeness which the child acquires in this relation comes under the category of what Lacan calls 'the Imaginary'. So also does the relationship of mother and child itself, in which the 'Desire of the Mother' represents both the mother's sense that the child will complete her desire, and the child's sense that the mother will complete its own.[48]

In the Oedipus Complex it is the father's threat of 'castration', consequent on the incest taboo, which intervenes on the child's desire for the mother. At this point the child leaves behind its pure immersion in the illusory realm of the Imaginary and enters the Symbolic Order, which is, most importantly, to enter language. For language is a system of differences, whose terms are defined relationally, and the phallus (though not the actual penis, but its representation) is the 'privileged signifier' of difference, in that its presence or absence is in question. Furthermore, just as the child's desire has to be deferred, in the Symbolic Order, until it can be deemed to be satisfied in adulthood, so its demand has to be expressed in the deferrals of language.

But the Imaginary persists in the ego's narcissistic illusions of wholeness and completeness, and enters into a dialectic with the Symbolic. Its delusions are put into question by the disturbing facts of the deferral of desire, and by the way desire and lack may speak against the subject's intentions in dreams, jokes, slips of the tongue. These are phenomena of the unconscious, and, by the same token, phenomena of the signifier. For the signifier is not the object, and represents its deferral. Lacan believes there is a fundamental instability in the relationship of signifier and signified. It is through the play permitted by this 'incessant sliding of the signified under the signifier'[49] that the unconscious is able to produce the formations of dreams, slips of the tongue, and so on. There is a split in the subject between the one that speaks and the one that thinks it speaks. The one that thinks it speaks is under the illusion that a secure Imaginary identity is guaranteed by what it sees as the fixity of its meaning (the signified). But the one that speaks is really subject to the infractions of desire in the signifier. The subject is thus split into the 'subject of the signified' and the 'subject of the signifier'.[50]

One area where the Imaginary most obviously seems to offer its consolations to the 'subject of the signified' is in the visual field, where Lacan identifies what he calls a 'scopic drive'. Desire invests itself in looking, seeking a wholeness in objects which may stand for the desired wholeness of the lost phallus. The subject's representation of this fantasy of wholeness is termed the *objet petit a*. But the look that seeks satisfaction here is not the same as the look that must submit to the Symbolic Order: there is 'the gaze' that pursues its fantasy, but there is also 'the eye' that is caught up in the Symbolic Order, reminded of lack and of the endlessness of the desire of the Other. So the dialectic of Symbolic

and Imaginary may manifest itself in a 'dialectic of the eye and the
gaze'.[51] Art exploits this dialectic in offering us a lure (the *trompe l'oeil*),
and a taming of the gaze (the *dompte-regard*). The taming, because art
tempers the fantasy by obtruding the facts of desire and lack into the
alluring field which had seemed to offer the complete satisfaction of the
union of ego and object.[52]

Lacanian theory may seem obviously relevant to literary criticism in at
least two areas: in providing a means of linking precise verbal effects to a
theory of the signifier which is also a theory of the self; and in analysing
constructions in the text which offer themselves as pictorial or descriptive, in relation to the 'eye' and and the 'gaze'.

Young's essay sees the represented split in Romantic consciousness as
a manifestation of the split described by Lacan. On this reading natural
objects become the *objet a*, offering, in the realm of the Imaginary, an
illusory healing of the split.

> It is the breech in the subject himself that the sound of waters seems to
> fill, offering a resolution of the dialectic of 'the impossible coincidence of
> the "I", the subject of the enunciation, with the "I", the subject of the
> utterance.' [Anika Lemaire. cf. subject of the signifier and subject of the
> signified.] In Wordsworth's myth, the sound of running water gives a
> wholeness like that of the infant, where no fracture has come to alienate
> being and meaning.[53]

'*Seems* to give a wholeness like that *imputed* to infants' might be a better
way of putting it. For *l'hommelette* is not 'whole'. And the relationship of
the mirror phase which follows is already alienated: the 'mirage' of
wholeness is given 'in an exteriority' which is 'in contrast with the
turbulent movements that the subject feels are animating him'.[54] But
there is a more worrying problem with Young's essay: it seems for a
moment to suggest, by identifying Wordsworth's split with Lacan's
concept, that the subject who writes the poem is identical with the
Symbolic subject, the subject of the signifier, who would thus be
privileged with complete insight into the Imaginary delusions, and the
unconsciously determined manifestations in the text. But nobody can
occupy this omniscient position, as far as Lacan is concerned: nobody is

'the subject who is supposed to know'.[55] Not that Young really believes this. And the whole of his essay is a salutary reminder that the resolution offered by Wordsworth is an Imaginary one. But for the sake of clarity it might be worth pointing out that 'the relatively self-conscious self' and the self presented as if restored by its encounter with Nature are both deeply implicated in the Imaginary: they correspond to the two poles of the alienated mirror relationship. The self that seeks or precedes restoration fears lack of meaning and seems to find it in an illusory completion and widening provided by an affinity with Nature. The primitive pattern of this process can be found, according to Lacan, in Freud's example of the *fort/da* game in *Beyond the Pleasure Principle*. The child holds a cotton reel attached to a thread, throws it out of the cot, and then hauls it back on its thread, saying *'fort'* ('gone') and *'da'* ('there'), thus seeking to master the disturbing fact of its mother's absence by a play on presence and absence controlled by itself. To the extent that the child is already submitted to desire and lack, and to the signification of difference (*fort/da*), this is a first entry into the Symbolic. But the mastery it assumes is illusory and comes under the category of the Imaginary. The game provides a primitive example of the dialectic of these two systems.

In Wordsworth's poetry the encounter with the Symbolic (a perspective, as we have noted, only offered after the threat of 'castration') occurs in those moments of faltering and threat to identity which accompany the sublime of Nature. But the concluding moment brings an illusory coherence. This corresponds to the idea of the poem as living letter: the impossible union of signifier and signified, which itself represents a healing of the split in the subject which had occurred with the acquisition of language. It is also a healing of the loss of the phallus: the full word is the phallic word.

Geoffrey Thurley's statement that Romantic subjectivity becomes part of the 'objective' is very perceptive. But it is too neat an idea, one that cannot do full justice to the ambitions of Romantic egotism. It remains better to prefer a model of oscillation between subject and object, albeit with a sharpened sense of what such terms imply, such as is advanced by Paul de Man in his essay 'Intentional Structure of the Romantic Image'.[56] This oscillation continues in the modern period.

IV

The transaction between mind and Nature takes place under the sign of the 'organic'. But the theory of the organic is unable to dispense with hints of the mechanical. Coleridge's formulations are notoriously ambiguous in this respect. As Pater said: 'What makes his view a one-sided one is, that in it the artist has become almost a mechanical agent: instead of the most luminous and self-possessed place of consciousness, the associative act in art or poetry is made to look like some blindly organic process of assimilation.'[57]

It is one of the best tributes to Shelley's intelligence that he made of the split between the experience of unity with Nature on the one hand, and the scientific (mechanical) explanations of Nature on the other, one of the subjects of his poetry. Shelley's sceptical mind plays around descriptions of natural phenomena which owe their origins to the scientific and deterministic outlook, as in the meteorological descriptions in 'Ode to the West Wind'. The imaginative intensity invested in these passages suggests that the 'mechanical' may be redeemed in the name of human wholeness; that Necessity (some of the links of which are uncovered by science) may, at its distant source, be conformable with the poetic intuitions of humanity. Yet looked at another way such a poem suggests that these intuitions themselves might be some pointless, inscrutable, mechanically determined effect of the unknown power which lies behind the West Wind.

Mary Shelley's *Frankenstein* makes a similar suggestion. It is noteworthy how often the monster appears in scenes which suggest a Wordsworthian conformity of Nature and the moral life. After learning of William's death, Frankenstein returns to Geneva, where a sublime thunderstorm breaks out over the Alps, 'so beautiful yet terrific' . . . 'This noble war in the sky elevated my spirits, I clasped my hands and exclaimed aloud, "William, dear angel! This is thy funeral, this thy dirge!"' At which point the artificial monster appears. A similar meeting occurs when Frankenstein contemplates 'the awful majesty' of Mont Blanc.

The monster has begun as a kind of Enlightenment child of Nature. Even then he is hideous, suggesting that the idea of a humanity whose causes are conceived in terms of mechanical necessity is itself hideous. And just as humanity may be depraved by its social environment, so the monster is depraved by his education: very much in accordance with Enlightenment polemics. Yet his proximity to settings of natural sub-limity implies that the causes of depravity themselves may stretch back to the workings of the awful and unknown power of the universe. Not that the myth thereby impugns that power itself as evil. Rather it raises the question whether, in being the source of both benevolent and depraved instincts, the unseen power might be indifferent to the moral feelings of humanity.

The mechanical, in its many guises, continues to afflict and disturb poets. Tennyson's 'Locksley Hall' depicts a little drama where the speaker, a young man of self-consciously rarefied sensibility, is jilted in favour of one who is rich, it seems, with the gains of a commerce relating to the growth of industry: industry as the castration of culture. And if the mechanical may occupy the most progressive nations, may this not be another sign of the kinship of humanity with mechanical processes, deriving from its source in an amoral and mechanical Neces-sity? Such an idea is entertained in Hardy's 'The Convergence of the Twain', on the loss of the *Titanic*. At a rather obvious level this poem concerns the inexorable workings of an inhuman chain of cause and effect:

> Well: while was fashioning
> This creature of cleaving wing
> The Immanent Will that stirs and urges everything . . .
>
> Prepared a sinister mate
> For her – so gaily great –
> A shape of ice, for the time far and dissociate.

And the indifference of the 'Immanent Will' to human purposes is as obvious in the effects of the disaster as in the disaster itself:

> Over the mirrors meant
> To glass the opulent
> The sea-worm crawls – grotesque, slimed, dumb, indifferent.

Yet the mechanical workings of the Immanent Will are reflected in the endeavours of humanity itself:

> Alien they seemed to be:
> No mortal eye could see
> The intimate welding of their later history.

Here the word 'welding' points to the mechanical processes that control both humanity and nature. This fact is related to the shape of the stanzas, which are like the shape of a ship. While such adjustment of stanzaic form derives its impulse from the idea of organic form, the fact that it imitates a machine merely reinforces the poem's message that organic processes, including the creation of poetry, are best seen as essentially mechanical:

> Steel chambers, late the pyres
> Of her salamandrine fires
> Cold currents thrid, and turn to rhythmic tidal lyres.

While this stanza points a piquant contrast between the rhythm of the ship's engine and that of the tide, it also posits the similarity on which that contrast is based, while the phrase 'rhythmic tidal lyres' specifically evokes the idea of poetry as a kind of rhythm which also owes its genesis to a determining necessity, of which the poet and his craft are more or less (depending on one's view of Hardy's 'fatalism') the slaves.

Hardy did not feel sanguine about the impersonality of this force. But Modernist poets, by contrast, have conducted an interesting manoeuvre with the organic *versus* mechanical opposition. They have tended to associate the mechanical with the empirical and the scientific, and the organic with emotivism, vagueness and all-obscuring personality. The organic becomes, in the view of male poets, the locus of an inferior feminine or effeminate mode. Modernist poets believe in the castrated condition of post-Romantic poetry, but claim that by contrast they can gain intuitive access to a mode of apprehension akin to that of the scientist: one which reveals, accurately and objectively, the true nature of things, in 'a machine made out of words', as William Carlos Williams puts it: a 'machine' inside which imagery derived from machines often functions as an index of power. The successors to the Modernists have another example, tending, though more ambiguously, in the same direction: that of the poets of the First World War, in whom precision-ism is allied with a punishment of supposed Romantic illusions and a presentation of the power of the destructive machine that occasionally takes on ambivalent sexual overtones.

The autonomy of objects, the presentation of the movement of the mind 'on the spot', the poem as living letter, the oscillation between subject and object – with the persistence of organicism in mechanical gear we have completed the inventory of modern debts to the nineteenth century required by the following pages. To these should be added the disavowal or disguise of those debts, and the characterization of Romantic-ism as marked by 'feminine' vagueness and sentimentality.

2

Ezra Pound

I

Pound's conversion to Imagism was certainly a bold transition, even if it was not instantaneous. It would be hard, from the poems collected in *Personae*, to predict the bracing severity of Pound's Imagist *dicta* in 'A Few Don'ts' or 'Prolegomena'.[1] The variety of styles, imitated from Victorians and Pre-Raphaelites, or acquired through translation, and the emotional freedom in the use of language, add up to an impression that is very far from suggesting Imagism, even if it may prepare us for other products of the later Pound.

Certain themes and attitudes, however, are constants, and have a bearing on the ideology of Imagism, and later developments of its concepts, even if they are not openly expressed in Pound's more Imagist poems. The most important array of ideas has to do with the presentation of a virile poet-persona, and with notions of the feminine implied by it. A poem which obviously illustrates this is 'Sestina: Altaforte', read aloud in a swashbuckling manner to a group of poets, and to the admiring Gaudier-Brzeska, in the Eiffel Tower restaurant in Soho. The poem concerns the troubadour Bertrans de Born. Pound had already made a connection of the troubadour cult with a celebration of masculine vitality and he must have made an identification of this mood

with his own virility: in 1913 he wrote to William Carlos Williams of
Gaudier-Brzeska, 'He is the only person with whom I can really be
"Altaforte".'² He probably thought of Gaudier's 'Hieratic Head' of him
in that light too: Wyndham Lewis used the word 'phallic' to describe
this sculpture.³ The poem begins in an aggressively Browningesque
manner, and celebrates war: 'Damn it all! all this our South stinks peace.
/ You whoreson dog, Papiols, come! Let's to music! / I have no life save
when the swords clash.' By contrast, the cowardly man is seen in
feminine terms:

> The man who fears war and squats opposing
> My words for stour, hath no blood of crimson
> But is fit only to rot in womanish peace
> Far from where worth's won and the swords clash.
> For the death of such sluts I go rejoicing.⁴

The word 'squats' here alludes to anatomical difference, and may also
contain an anal allusion, as Peter Makin suggests, thus pointing forward
to later connections of the anal and the feminine in Pound's work.⁵

But there is something of a willed assumption of the mask of virility
about this and other similar Pound poems; and there is a concomitant
sense of insecurity and anxiety which is also to be a persistent strain in
his work. Moving on to *Ripostes* one sees a lack of firm identity being
associated with a woman in 'Portrait d'une Femme':

> Your mind and you are our Sargasso Sea.
> London has swept about you this score years
> And bright ships left you this or that in fee:
> Ideas, old gossip, oddments of all things,
> Strange spars of knowledge and dimmed wares of price . . .
> No! there is nothing! In the whole and all,
> Nothing that's quite your own.
> Yet this is you.

This could well be a description of Pound's own sojourn in London.
Compare the way he projects his sense of drift there onto Mauberley in
1920:

A consciousness disjunct,
Being but this overblotted
Series
Of intermittences;

Coracle of Pacific voyages,
The unforecasted beach;
Then on an oar
Read this:

'I was
And I no more exist;
Here drifted
An hedonist.'

                                                    'Mauberley', IV

And in Canto I, which may be seen as an allegory of Pound's escape from London, we are reminded of Elpenor, 'A man of no fortune and with a name to come', dying in the long voyage home from Troy while descending a ladder in Circe's house. London is associated, in Hugh Selwyn Mauberley, with the distractions of Odysseus' voyage home: there is the reference in 'E. P. Ode Pour L'Election de son Sépulchre' to the Sirens and to Circe. But even Odysseus, the hero with whom Pound identified, may represent the loss of firm identity, for the Cantos often repeat the wily reply he gave to the Cyclops when asked his name: οὖτις: 'Nobody'. The repetition suggests the receptiveness of the Cantos, their frequent impersonality. But on the basis of many of Pound's other poems, including parts of the Cantos, and 'Sestina Altaforte' one would see an equally strong tendency towards the assertion of firm personality, or the admiration of it in others. In 'Portrait d'une Femme' Pound is anxiously projecting his own sense of drift, directionlessness, and subjection to diverse influences, onto the safe, and to him appropriate, figure of a woman.

Pound makes a constant association of the directing intelligence with the male. This is worth bearing in mind as one reads the Imagist propositions expounded in 'A Few Don'ts' and 'Prolegomena' even though they do not seem to raise questions of gender in any obvious way. For the connection of Poundian clarity with masculinity is an important one, as will become clearer. Meanwhile, there are other things to observe about these propositions; and about the further remarks Pound adds to them when he gathers them together in 'A Retrospect'. These latter read:

1 Direct treatment of the 'thing' whether subjective or objective.
2 To use absolutely no word that does not contribute to the presentation.
3 As regarding rhythm: to compose in the sequence of the musical phrase, not in sequence of a metronome.[6]

As Alan Durant points out, these propositions treat language as a transparent medium for registering objects or experiences apprehended by a subject who is conceived as 'external to and pre-existing language'. They subordinate signifier to signified, and evade the materiality of language.[7] Whatever liberating force they may have had in their time, or may still possess, they also offer opportunities for a coercive poetics and a limited and ahistorical poetry. The third proposition, regarding rhythm, may seem to evade these strictures to some degree, but from one of the original discussions (in 'Credo') it is clear that, whatever 'the musical phrase' may be, it derives from the idea of the unique perceptions of the individual subject, and assigns to language an ancillary role:

Rhythm – I believe in an 'absolute rhythm', a rhythm, that is, in poetry, which corresponds exactly to the emotion or shade of emotion to be expressed. A man's rhythm must be interpretative, it will be, therefore, in the end, his own, uncounterfeiting, uncounterfeitable.[8]

This passage also introduces another theme: the idea of language as, albeit ancillary to the subject's perceptions, essentially *voice* or *speech*: a suggestion of the immediate presence of meaning to the subject, and an elision of the disruption, contradictions and polyvalency imposed by the difference and deferral of the signifying chain.

There are other features of these propositions which deserve attention. The association of the poet with the scientist is a recurring theme in Pound, and one which is also popular with other Modernist poets:

Consider the way of the scientists rather than the way of an advertising agent for a new soap.

> The scientist does not expect to be acclaimed as a great scientist until he has *discovered* something.[9]

The comparison with the scientist has at least three purposes: first, to lend greater authority to the poet's perceptions and pronouncements; secondly, to validate the idea of literature as experimentation; thirdly, to set the Modernist apart from Romantic organicism. Modernist poets struggle with organicism like flies in jelly. It is open to question whether or not anyone has ever escaped. But the need to rebel is not in question. As Pound says in 'Credo':

> As for the nineteenth century, with all respect to its achievements, I think we shall look back upon it as a rather blurry, messy sort of a period, a rather sentimentalistic, mannerish sort of a period ...
>   As to Twentieth century poetry, and the poetry which I expect to see written during the next decade or so, it will, I think, move against poppy-cock, it will be harder and saner, it will be what Mr. Hewlett calls 'nearer the bone'. It will be as much like granite as it can be ... We will have fewer painted adjectives impeding the shock and stroke of it. At least for myself, I want it so, austere, direct, free from emotional slither.[10]

One might begin to suspect that the opposition between 'hardness', 'directness', science, and 'a man's rhythm' on the one hand, and sentiment, blur, mess, 'painted adjectives' and 'emotional slither' on the other, conceals a set of values related to gender. This is certainly the case, as we shall see.

The analogy with science is also important for understanding Pound's sense of what the poem is and not just the role of the poet. Some of the implications of the analogy mitigate the sense of coercion and closure evinced by Pound's Imagist axioms. But others do not.

In 'The Serious Artist' (1913) Pound announces that 'Bad art is inaccurate art. It is art that makes false reports. If a scientist falsifies a report either deliberately or through negligence we consider him as either a criminal or a bad scientist according to the enormity of his offence.'[11] The scientific analogy is used in the service of the ideal of the precise rendering of the 'thing': 'The touchstone of an art is its precision.' Such precision is the gift of the good artist: it is partly a matter of

'control' ('"Good writing" is perfect control'), partly a matter of the
artist's 'energy' transmitted by the work. The good artist contains this
energy because he is living in the correct relationship to the cosmos and
to his own sexuality. Certainly Pound was, by 1921, capable of com-
paring the brain to genital fluid.[12]

Nevertheless, the notion of the poem itself as a battery of energy has
potentially liberating implications. The idea is described in 'The Serious
Artist':

> We might come to believe that the thing that matters in art is a sort of
> energy, something more or less like electricity or radioactivity, a force
> transfusing, welding, and unifying. A force rather like water when it
> spurts up through very bright sand and sets it in swift motion . . .
>   What is the difference between poetry and prose?
>   I believe that poetry is the more highly energized.[13]

This conception suggests the dynamic, unlike the Imagist formulations,
even though the energy is subject to the 'perfect control' of the artist.
Despite the Romantic organicism of such a balance of energy and
control, Pound delighted in the scientific air of the concept. He probably derived it from Hudson Maxim's book, *The Science of Poetry and the
Philosophy of Language* which he reviewed in 1910. There it is argued
that 'Poetry obeys the law of conservation of energy. By poetry a
thought is presented with the utmost economy of word symbols.'[14]
Several features of Maxim's book particularly suggest a dynamic conception of the poem, and clearly exercised some influence on Pound in the
working out of his own versions of the vortex and the ideogram. One is
the idea of 'interactivities', which are forces of relationship that are more
important than the things that are related.[15] Another is the importance
placed on the verb, for the reason that 'poetry must always be greatest
when it exists in action.'[16] Both of these notions find precise echoes in
Fenollosa; the first in his assertion that 'Relations are more real and more
important than the things which they relate;'[17] the second in his discussion of the noun and the verb:

> A true noun, an isolated thing, does not exist in nature. Things are only
> the terminal points, or rather the meeting points, of actions, cross-

sections cut through actions, snapshots. Neither can a pure verb, an abstract motion, be possible in nature. The eye sees noun and verb as one: things in motion, motion in things, and so the Chinese conception tends to represent them.[18]

Given his interest in scientific analogies, it is not surprising that Pound should compare Fenollosa's description of 'lines of force' between nouns and verbs with the lines of force in the field theories of physics. Nor that he should relate the explanation of lines of force in terms of molecular vortices, given by Clark Maxwell, to his own conception of the vortex.[19] All of these ideas considerably complicate any description that would seek to depict Pound as the static observer of static 'things'.

What about the vortex itself? It is chiefly intended as an image which will describe both the activity of the artist's consciousness and the properties of the work of art itself. It consists of a central rod, or wire, into which adjacent energies are constantly rushing. The rod is the poet's consciousness, organizing adjacent ideas and experiences. It therefore does not entirely depart from the Imagist conception of a subject separate from its experiences, recording them through a language whose proper function is to act as a transparent medium. The central rod has obvious phallic connotations, and suggests the idea of control.

The vortex itself impregnates the 'passive vulva' of London;[20] 'ALL MOMENTUM, which is the past bearing upon us / RACE, RACE-MEMORY, instinct charging the PLACID, / NON-ENERGIZED FUTURE'.[21] In a letter to John Quinn, Pound describes his admiring response to another vorticist, Wyndham Lewis:

> The vitality, the fullness of the man ... beauty, heaven, hell, sarcasm, every kind of whirlwind of force and emotion. Vortex. That is the right word, if I did find it myself. Every kind of geyser from jism bursting as white as ivory, to hate or a storm at sea. Spermatozoon, enough to repopulate the island with active and vigorous animals.[22]

Wyndham Lewis as Moby Dick? In 'Affirmations II: Vorticism', Pound contrasts the force of the vortex with the 'charming' automatic paintings of Florence Seth, which are *organic*; he suggests a hierarchy, with vorticism at the top and at the bottom the 'vegetable or visceral memory' which is at work in Miss Seth's paintings.[23] Here the equations are complete. Vortex: male: energy; organicism: female: passivity.

Yet at the same time the image of the vortex is ambiguous, for a vortex has no perceptible centre, and the organization that occurs may seem to derive from some unconscious energy which allows the adjacent ideas to generate their own significance. This would indeed correspond to Pound's avowed ideal of juxtaposition without comment. Yet since he clearly values that perceptiveness and *virtù* in the artist which can see clearly 'things' and, of course, their relations, the idea of control remains lurking behind the ambiguous image of the vortex. It is precisely because of the serious artist's perceptiveness and control that the energies presented in poetry can take on significance in juxtaposition without any intrusive comment: '"Good writing" is perfect control. And it is quite easy to control a thing that has no energy.'[24] And more difficult to control a thing that does have energy, especially if your ability to express that energy is an index of the energy in yourself. But despite the heavy implied compliment to the artist and his control, in practice the writing of poetry may become a more uncertain business when conducted under the sign of the vortex than it was under the sign of the Image.

Pound's understanding of the ideogram exhibits the same ambiguity. Certainly one attraction of the ideogram was the pictorial element, which suggested a direct relationship with the thing. But equally Pound was impressed by the combination of several such elements in one character: juxtaposition again. Further, the fact that Chinese ideograms were not in fact pictograms but economical reductions suggested that analytic approach to the object to be found in vorticist graphic art. Pound was impressed by Gaudier's ability to read certain ideograms at sight. This certainly indicates a responsiveness to the pictorial element. But it equally suggests a kinship between the reduction of the object in the ideogram and the analytical reduction of the object into planes in vorticist graphic art. The instant apprehension of the relation of character and thing seems less a matter of control than of some instinctive virtue. But the vorticist reduction, with its machine-tooled appearance, has the attraction of scientific precision and control.

Pound not only saw control as important, but had ideas about the effect it would have on the work of art. He spoke of metaphor as interpretative: the poet 'must prepare for new advances along the lines of true metaphor, that is interpretative metaphor, or image, and diametrically opposed to untrue, or ornamental metaphor.'[25] In this assertion the word 'true' implies not only that this is metaphor proper, but that it is 'true' to the 'thing' – since, as we have seen, accuracy is incumbent on the artist. So here again we have the same ambiguity: is the artist imposing an interpretation, or guiding the truth? It is not easy to see precisely how metaphor can be true to the thing. Perhaps by exhibiting a structure in the vehicle which is consonant with that in the supposed tenor. Or perhaps by signalling that it is leaving the thing alone. The latter view is taken by some contemporary Poundians, who (unlike Pound) often appear to be hostile to metaphor itself, and who attempt to interpret Pound's statements in accordance with this prejudice.[26]

Thus, in discussing Pound's remarks above on metaphor, Laszlo K. Géfin has this to say:

> The image interprets; it does not interpose or encroach. In the 'Metro' poem, the apparition of the faces *is not* a black bough with petals. In the ideogrammatic composition the mind *re-creates*, or rather *creates*, in accordance with nature's processes; it tries not to 'break the universe'. Such metaphoric juxtapositions evince a reticence on the part of the poet, an unwillingness to tamper with reality.[27]

Note how these remarks reiterate the Poundian divorce of poet and reality, a divorce which is itself very apparent in the poem in question, 'In a Station of the Metro'. The original published form of this was as follows:

The apparition	of these faces	in the crowd:
Petals	on a wet, black	bough.

The observation of spaces between the rhythmic units invites an attention to each separate idea which is analogous to that invited by a Chinese ideogram. Despite Pound's reverence for the verb, this is a poem of noun-substantives: noun-substantives we are forced to see as unrelated, except, ironically enough, in so far as the juxtaposition of the two lines invites a kind of equation, represented by the colon (later changed to a semi-colon) – ironically, because Géfin has asked us to see the Poundian image as reticent and unobtrusive. Now there is no simple way of avoiding the description of this poem as metaphorical. And among tortuous ways of describing the poem as metaphorical in a new fashion Géfin's assertion that 'the apparition of the faces *is not* a black bough' seems remarkably threadbare. When were the things compared in a metaphor ever identical with each other? What Géfin interprets as a formal feature of the new Poundian metaphor is really an effect of other features of the poem: the distance of the bough from the crowd; its *hokku*-like brevity, suggesting a very simple juxtaposition; the sense of capturing, as Pound said of this very poem, 'the precise instant when a thing outward and objective transforms itself or darts into a thing inward and subjective'.[28] Everything about the poem, in fact, that suggests the alienation of an isolated subject responding to a world of supposedly separate objectivity. The social reality of the big city is here aestheticized and dehistoricized.[29] For the Imagist programme certainly renders the interpretation and explanation of history difficult, in that it requires any general sense not only to be expressed in vivid particular perceptions, but also to emerge from the apprehension of particulars. Yet, while noting the tendency of the 'Metro' poem, it would be unfair to suggest that the *Cantos* (the avowed aim of which is to explain history) are marked by such incapacity – and not only for the obvious but important reason that they constitute a long poem. For the *Cantos* consist of large, juxtaposed blocks of verse (making large ideograms) and no two blocks can be reduced to the equation, objective: subjective. Rather they correspond to the idea of juxtaposed objectivities. Nevertheless, they are saddled with the problem of making historical sense emerge from particulars.

Let it merely be said that Pound's Imagist phase is indeed marked by the static and alienated quality his pronouncements might lead one to expect, and that there is no reason to take seriously any suggestion from either Pound or his followers that a new type of metaphor is present at this stage in his work.

But what of the ideogrammatic method of the *Cantos*? Here the juxtaposed blocks of verse correspond to components of a composite ideogram. The beginning of Canto IV provides a good example of the method, close to the start of the *Cantos*, and moreover one that exhibits some of their most important preoccupations:

> Palace in smoky light,
> Troy but a heap of smouldering boundary stones,
> ANAXIFORMINGES! Aurunculeia!

Hear me. Cadmus of Golden Prows!
The silver mirrors catch the bright stones and flare,
Dawn, to our waking, drifts in the green cool light;
Dew-haze blurs, in the grass, pale ankles moving.
Beat, beat, whirr, thud, in the soft turf
     under the apple trees,
  Choros nympharum, goat-foot, with the pale foot alternate;
  Crescent of blue-shot waters, green-gold in the shallows,
  A black cock crows in the sea-foam.[30]

The first twleve lines present images of the rise and fall of great
civilizations: the fall of Troy; the founding of Thebes (by 'Cadmus of
Golden Prows' the grandfather of Dionysus). Juxtaposed with these are
ideas and images of love: 'Aurunculeia' is the bride of Manlius, and she
is the subject of Catullus' epithalamion; 'Dawn, to our waking . . .'
presents two lovers in the early morning; 'choros nympharum, goat-foot,
with the pale foot alternate' is reminiscent of some Dionysian festival,
satyrs dancing with nymphs. A third level of meaning extends from
'ANAXIFORMINGES' ('Lords of the Lyre': Pindar, *Olympian* II): a
reference to poetry and music.

    These juxtapositions add up to a sense of the immemorial inter-
dependence of civilization, poetry and love. Also the dangers as well as
the beauty of passion, especially when one remembers that the fall of
Troy was brought about by the love of Paris for Helen. The ensuing
lines confirm and extend the impression. An old man tells tales of love,
starting with the cry, (l. 16) 'Ityn!', which refers to Itys, the son of
Procne, who was the wife of Tereus, king of Thrace. He raped Procne's
sister, Philomela, and cut out her tongue. The sisters revenged themselves by killing Itys and serving him up to Tereus in a dish. When
Tereus discovered that he had eaten his own son, he attempted to kill
them, but they were changed into birds (it is usually said, into a
swallow and a nightingale). The Provençal story of the troubadour
Cabestan (Guillen da Cabestan), which follows (ll. 21 ff), is that he fell
in love with the Lady Soremonda. Her husband killed him in jealousy
and served his heart up cooked. Soremonda vowed never to eat again and
committed suicide by throwing herself from a window.

    Actaeon (ll. 33 ff), changed into a stag by Diana because he had seen
her bathing, was also the grandson of Cadmus. He was torn to pieces by
hunting-dogs. Piere Vidal (1175 – 1215), another troubadour (ll. 52 – 4),

fell in love with the Lady Loba ('she-wolf') and was driven to madness: he dressed in wolfskins and ran wild in the woods, where he was hunted by dogs. All these stories point to the overpowering force of passion, its power to transform (metamorphosis) and its potential for destruction: literally for dismemberment: loss of identity. The phrase "Tis. 'Tis. Ytis' (1.32) is at one and the same time the name 'Itys' supposedly repeated by the swallow; an affirmation of the destructive power of love as being in the nature of things ('It is' as answering the Lady Soremonda's 'It is Cabestan's heart in the dish?' (1.22)); and a repetition of Odysseus' assumed name οὗτις ('Nobody'); a reminder that loss of identity is a constant theme of the *Cantos*.

Such loss of identity may be salutary: a divine frenzy, born of the pure light of love which intrudes into these lines of Canto IV at several points, as in the image of the self-generated light of Diana's hair, shining in total darkness (ll.40−51). This frenzy and this light are especially associated in Pound's mind with the Dionysian ritual, which he thought was central to the Eleusinian mysteries, vestiges of which he felt sure had survived into Provence.[31] Pound feels ambivalent about loss of identity: the wine of Bacchus, frenzy, the clouding of intelligence, must not be sought after. They come as an adjunct of love, the operation of which ultimately serves intelligence. When courted as a means of escape their proper image lies in the spells of the enchantress Circe, who also figures largely in the *Cantos*.

This discussion has served merely to indicate how the ideogrammatic method works at a relatively local level, and at the same time to introduce some of the leading ideas of the *Cantos* in a convenient way. The ideogrammatic method, however, is intended to function on a larger scale as well. Thus when reading Canto IV one may bear in mind Canto III with its initial evocation of divine light underlying the beauty of modern Venice; and Canto I, with its memories of escape from Circe, and its description of a rite propitiating Pluto and Persephone, who, it seems, Pound saw as impregnated by Dionysus.

II

The items here juxtaposed correspond to the 'arrangement of planes' or 'planes in relation' Pound saw in Vorticist art.[32] The 'lines of relation' between these 'planes' correspond to what, at the thematic level, is presented as 'metamorphosis'. Nature is a protean process, whose prime validating moment is the luminous moment of love, when one is transformed into a god, or perceives in a godlike manner:

> What is a god?
> A god is an eternal state of mind ...
> When is a god manifest?
> When the states of mind take form.
> When does a man become a god?
> When he enters one of these states of mind.[33]

Such a state of mind is present in Canto IV in the lines succeeding 'Dawn to our waking ...' and in Actaeon's perception of Diana bathing. The fact that this substitute for the transcendent appears in such a moment of luminous perception validates the method of luminous details in general: Nature is a process passing through particular but variable, multiple and open-ended shapes, governed by the sexual power of love. That power may make itself felt to those who respond to the process, rather than imposing the linear and rigid constraints of logical thinking. As Fenollosa says:

> Logic cannot deal with any kind of interaction or with any multiplicity of function ... For it the poor neglected things at the bases of pyramids are only so many particulars or pawns.
>   Science fought till she got at the things ... Poetry agrees with science and not with logic.[34]

Poetry responds to things and the relations between them. Its metaphors are reflections of the lines of relation in nature: 'primitive metaphors do not spring from arbitrary subjective processes. They are possible only because they follow objective lines of relation in nature herself.'[35] Language should therefore seek to correspond to the order of these lines of relation, and in doing so it may jettison logic, and, Pound thinks, syntax. At the same time it will cultivate metaphor, which is the figure of speech that corresponds to metamorphosis.

As far as the *Cantos* are concerned, the most important form of metaphor is that which denotes an equivalence between two juxtaposed items – for example between Actaeon's being changed into a stag and hunted, and Vidal's dressing as a wolf and being hunted. What is 'interpretative' about metaphor is that the poet is able to see clearly the relations that subsist. Pound's *periplum*, or Odyssean voyage around the shores (or visible edges) of history, asks us to accept that he has a privileged access to the details which demonstrate the eternal recurrence of the same conception of sexual love, and its importance for the arts and the good governance of society. Poets who share this access are indeed 'the antennae of the race', then, and society cannot function without them: 'the individual cannot act effectively or frame his thought, the governor and legislator cannot act effectively or frame his laws, without words, and the solidity and validity of these words is the care of the damned and despised *litterati.*'[36] The whole conception – whether looked at from the point of view of the vortex or that of the role of the poet with respect to words – surreptitiously reasserts the authority, indeed the authoritarianism, of the poet, even as it seems to portray him responding sensitively to particulars. The role of the (male) poet is akin to that of 'the governor', and the governor must be 'a male of the species', as Pound described Mussolini. In *Hugh Selwyn Mauberley* the turpitude of the modern age is described in these terms:

> All men, in law, are equals.
> Free of Pisistratus,
> We choose a knave or an eunuch
> To rule over us.

In Canto LIV the right order of things under the 4th Dynasty (Tsin) is threatened by eunuchs, who become the powers behind the throne, singing 'emptiness is the beginning of all things.'[37] This emptiness, or fundamental lack, is often consciously portrayed as the lack of the phallus in Pound's work. But in the Usura Cantos the lack of the lost object becomes the appalling, unstoppable loss of the faeces or excrement, symbolically brought about by the inflation consequent on usury. Maud Ellmann has noted that Freud linked parsimony with anal retention.[38] Equally he noted that 'In the products of the unconscious the concepts *faeces* (money, gift) *baby* and *penis* are ill-distinguished from one another and are easily interchangeable.'[39] The loss of the phallus may therefore be represented by the metaphor of the loss of the faeces. Lacan notes that, 'the anal level is the locus of metaphor – one object for another, give the faeces in place of the phallus.'[40] Metaphor is itself the figure that arises on entry into the Symbolic, when the signifier, the Name of the Father, is given in place of the lack. Pound's horrified recognition that the word may never be adequate to the thing finds its expression in the metaphors of the overproduction of excrement and the inflation of money.[41] Value no longer relates to commodities or labour: words no longer apply to things: 'When the application of word to thing goes rotten, i.e. becomes slushy and inexact, or excessive or bloated, the whole machinery of social and individual thought and order goes to pot. This is a lesson of history.'[42]

The law of the phallus and phallic sexuality enjoins the application of word to thing and the rule of a male governor, who, like the Chinese Emperor, has the 'mandate of heaven', making him an image of the sky-god on earth. This right ordering ensures the continuance of fertility ('Zeus lies in Ceres' bosom', Canto LXXI). Against this law stand usury, contraception, sodomy and, in art, the 'mushy technique' which divorces words from things. Metaphor, following Lacan, we may see as the figure of repression, the figure by virtue of which in the entry to the Symbolic, one signifier stands in for another; according to 'the Name of the Father' the signifier stands for the lost object, the phallus. It is fitting, there-fore, that the endless equivalences of Pound's *Cantos* are always in the end equivalent to phallic sexuality, and fitting also that the hysterical disavowal of difference and of castration should accompany them. In the end, every 'luminous detail' is Eleusis. And Eleusis is surrounded by Circe and sodomy. It is very wrong to see Pound's 'preference', with Marjorie Perloff, as being 'for the metonymic over the metaphoric function'.[43] Indeed, in accordance with Pound's ambivalence as between control and receptivity, with the accent on control, one might say that the effect of the *Cantos* is to look metonymic while being metaphoric. Yet that would be too crude a summary. Metonymy, in that it endlessly refers the subject along the signifying chain, in quest of the deferred lost object, is the figure of desire. And it is worth looking in more detail at the manner in which desire inflicts itself both on Pound's ambivalent theories and on the practice of his poetry.

Woman appears in Canto XLVII in the context of Odysseus' encoun-ter with Circe:

Two span, two span to a woman
Beyond that she believes not. Nothing is of any importance.
. . .
The stars are not in her counting
To her they are but wandering holes.[44]

The intelligence of the wily Odysseus computes and orders the movements of the stars; but woman represents the endlessness and lack of
fixity of desire. Her understanding of the stars is reducible to her status
as wandering and as a hole: for the epithet may indeed be transferred
from the stars to her. Yet the 'hole' may reappear elsewhere with a
positive value. Thus, in one of his letters he asserts: 'I do NOT want
"Tos Temps" sung in a translation. The HOLE point of my moozik bein
that the moozik fits the WORDS and not some OTHER WORDS.'[45]
The description of the 'HOLE point' is strikingly apposite for the vortex
itself, which as we have seen can be looked at as both ordering and
receptive. But here the intention is to guard the irreducible fitness of
words and rhythm to the experience. Yet the misspelling HOLE suggests that the corrosive effects of translation are somewhere perceived by
Pound as having invaded the centre of his project. And why should they
not? For the *Cantos*, from the very start, are an overlayered work of
translation. The immediate relation of word and thing, immediate
presence, is everywhere called into question by Pound's actual practice.
There is no more convenient example of this than Canto I which
translates Andreas Divus's Latin translation from the *Odyssey* into the
quasi-Anglo-Saxon mode of *The Seafarer* – a mode which might be
dubbed 'translatorese', albeit of an admirable kind. Elsewhere, Pound's
habit of giving the documents straight, as for instance in vast tracts of
the China Cantos, while it presents itself as a kind of empiricism, in
reality obtrudes the fact of discourse between the reader and the 'thing'.
    Even the image of excrement may be subject to a reversal of values. In
the *Guide to Kulchur* Pound announces: '*Vortex is energy!* and it gave forth
solid excrements in the quattro & cinque cento, *liquid* until the seven-
teenth century, *gases* whistle till now.'[46] Here the anal decline from
well-formed Renaissance excrement to late Romantic flatulence gives a
positive value to solid excrement, and lends support to the view that
excrement, in becoming a metaphor for the lost object, emphasizes that
loss in its over-production. Well-formed loss on the other hand, does

not provoke such anxiety. Nevertheless the image is reversible: some-where Pound realizes that poetry is not identical with the expression of a unified voice.

III

The proliferation of the word in pursuit of desire leaves its mark in more ways than one. The *Cantos* are not all of a piece. And certainly later sections of the work do seem to have a more metonymic character than earlier ones. Marjorie Perloff offers one of the Pisan Cantos, Canto LXXXI, as an example of this. Here are the first twelve lines:

> Zeus lies in Ceres' bosom
> Taishan is attended of loves
>   under Cythera, before sunrise
> and he said: 'Hay aquí mucho catolicismo – (sounded catoli*th*ismo)
>   y muy poco reliHion'
> and he said: 'Yo creo que los reyes desaparecen'
> (Kings will, I think, disappear)
> That was Padre José Elizondo
>   in 1906 and in 1917
> or about 1917
>   and Dolores said: 'Come pan, niño,' eat bread, me lad

There are obvious associations of love, fertility and the cosmic and social order: 'Zeus lies in Ceres' bosom' is another example from Pound's inventory of fertility myths, while at the same time it denotes that there are low rain-clouds over the camp at Pisa where he is held prisoner after his capture by the Americans. Taishan is the sacred mountain of China where the Great Emperor of the Eastern Peak lived. The Emperor is a living expression of the sky-god. The theme of fertility surfaces in a less obvious way with Dolores: '"Come pan, niño," eat bread, me lad.' This owner of a pension in Madrid becomes a kind of earth-mother, an incarnation of Ceres.

But other elements in the canto are hard to clamp into any overriding structure. Pound's friend, Claude G. Bowers, for instance, appears in line 22 because memories of Spain have figured largely. One might see his remark, 'But such hatred, / I had never conceived such', (ll. 22 – 3) which refers to the Spanish Communists in the Civil War, as reflecting the fascist aspect of Pound's myth. And one might not. It is certainly not coerced into that role, however, and the overriding accent of this passage, and many others in the Pisan Cantos, is on the associative, the metonymic. In so far as there is closure, the resurgence of the old metaphors, this is hardly surprising, for short of total insanity, the drive to coherence cannot be suspended. Pound, in the Pisan Cantos, takes association of ideas as far from closure as is perhaps possible. Here the other side of his ambivalent formulae is granted expression: the receptive.

And it is not only by virtue of that associative method that *The Cantos* delight in the disseminative play of the signifier. For Pound's use of language by no means adheres to the puritanism his pronouncements exact. In 'How to Read' Pound had isolated three 'kinds of poetry':

MELOPOEIA, wherein the words are charged, over and above their plain meaning, with some musical property, which directs the bearing or trend of that meaning.

PHANOPOEIA, which is a casting of images upon the visual imagination.

LOGOPOEIA, 'the dance of the intellect among words', that is to say, it employs words not only for their direct meaning, but it takes count in a special way of habits of usage, of the context we *expect* to find with the word, its usual concomitants, of its known acceptances, and of ironical play.[47]

It is this third category which is perhaps surprising in the light of Pound's other utterances. Yet it indicates what he admired in Laforgue:

He is the finest wrought; he is most 'verbalist'. Bad verbalism is rhetoric, or the use of *cliché* unconsciously, or a mere playing with phrase. But there is good verbalism, distinct from lyricism or imagism, and in this Laforgue is a master. He writes not the popular language of any country but an international tongue common to the excessively cultivated.[48]

Pound himself used *logopoeia* most consistently in *Homage to Sextus Propertius*. Consider the beginning of that poem:

Shades of Callimachus, Coan ghosts of Philetas
It is in your grove I would walk,
I who come first from the clear font
Bringing the Grecian orgies into Italy,
            and the dance into Italy.
Who hath taught you so subtle a measure,
            in what hall have you heard it;
What foot beat out your time-bar,
            what water has mellowed your whistles?

Out-weariers of Apollo will, as we know, continue their Martian
    generalities,
            We have kept our erasers in order.
A new-fangled chariot follows the flower-hung horses;
A young Muse with young loves clustered about her
            ascends with me into the aether, . . .
And there is no high-road to the Muses.

Annalists will continue to record Roman reputations,
Celebrities from the Trans-Caucasus will belaud Roman celebrities
And expound the distentions of Empire,
But for something to read in normal circumstances?
For a few pages brought down from the forked hill unsullied?
I ask a wreath which will not crush my head.
            And there is no hurry about it;
I shall have, doubtless, a boom after my funeral,
Seeing that long standing increases all things regardless of quality.

Apart from the superb rhythmic cadence of this, which it is not our
purpose to discuss here, one might note the piquant collocation of lyrical
intensity in the first verse-paragraph with the cosmopolitan, cultivated
urbanity that follows: 'Out-weariers of Apollo will, as we know, continue their Martian generalities.' Irony: 'We have kept our erasers in
order.' And ironic use of cliché: 'I shall have, doubtless, a boom after my
funeral.' *Homage to Sextus Propertius* is an attempt, largely successful, to
present the very civilized consciousness of late imperial Britain, and it
plainly delights in a polyphonic discursiveness which cannot easily be
incorporated into an empiricist poetic. It should not really need saying
that the same is true of *The Cantos*, since so many parts show it.
Demonstration would be otiose and banal. Even the graphic effects,

intended to convey the desired fit of word and thing, only succeed in setting up a disjunction between the vocal and the written which calls into question the desired immediate presence of the poet's voice, with its 'absolute rhythm'. For the graphic effects, whether of placing on the page or the writing of an ideogram, cannot be fitted, with anything approaching exactness, to the idea of expressive voice. Of course, Pound would have liked the idea that records of his spoken performances should be regarded as canonical texts. But this attitude only serves to obscure certain genuinely radical aspects of Pound's poem. It is certainly ludicrous for a critic such as Antony Easthope, who claims to be strongly influenced by Derrida, to end up arguing for such an approach, not only because of its blatant phonocentrism, but also because the very idea of a canonical text smacks of a repressive intentionalism.[49]

It is doubtful whether one should speak of this as 'the Pound era'. This is an imperialistic and very Poundian gesture which invites one to ignore and belittle the many currents in contemporary poetry on both sides of the Atlantic which owe little to the Poundian aesthetic, whether in its totalitarian or libertarian aspects. Yet, as Bunting said of the *Cantos*:

> There they are, you will have to go a long way round
> if you want to avoid them.
> It takes some getting used to. There are the Alps,
> fools! Sit down and wait for them to crumble![50]

Despite the repressive aspects of Pound's theories, and the closure effected in his Imagist poems, he moves a long way, consciously and unconsciously, towards a liberated poetic of desire. In the end he transcends the limiting tendencies of his own doctrines. When he complained of *The Cantos* that he could not 'make it cohere', he only showed how deep was his adherence to organicism, for all the scientific posturing. Yet he himself, at other times, showed a preference for a more open form of organicism: the tradition, deriving also from Romanticism, of the fragmentary and unfinished. If he liked Gaudier's 'Hieratic Head' for its phallic suggestion, he equally admired its unfinished quality. And one thing he was ready to praise Whitman for was that 'he never pretended to have reached the goal'[51] Pound's practice provides the basis for a rich and polyvalent poetry. To escape from its entanglement in organicist aesthetics it would have required some theory of the subject and its discourses as historical. But as the basis for a new and adventurous poetic there is no better place to start than with Pound. And the motto should be, 'Do as Pound does, not as he says.'

3

T. S. ELIOT

I

The 'objective' makes its most obvious appearance in Eliot's criticism in the form of 'the objective correlative', in the essay 'Hamlet and his Problems':

> The only way of expressing emotion in the form of art is by finding an 'objective correlative'; in other words, a set of objects, a situation, a chain of events which shall be the formula of that *particular emotion*; such that when the external facts, which must terminate in sensory experience are given, the emotion is immediately evoked ... The artistic 'inevitability' lies in this complete adequacy of the external to the emotion; and this is precisely what is deficient in *Hamlet*. Hamlet (the man) is dominated by an emotion which is inexpressible, because it is in *excess* of the facts as they appear. And the supposed identity of Hamlet with his author is genuine to this point: that Hamlet's bafflement at the absence of objective equivalent to his feelings is a prolongation of the bafflement of his creator in the face of his artistic problem. Hamlet is up against the difficulty that his disgust is occasioned by his mother, but that his mother is not an adequate equivalent for it; his disgust envelops and exceeds her.[1]

It is important to be clear about what this passage is saying, and what are its implications.

First, it accords primacy in art to the expression of emotion, a

post-Romantic priority. The purpose of the 'objective correlative' or 'set
of objects' is to achieve this aim successfully and in a manner that can be
represented as dispassionate, in accordance with modern notions of the
aesthetic. Secondly, there is some ambiguity about the 'objective correlative': is it chiefly the 'external facts' as more or less outside the work in
some sense? Or is it, on the other hand, the presentation of those 'facts'
in art? In any case, an important emphasis does rest on the latter
conception: the artist has to render the external into a 'formula' which
will evoke the correct emotion. But thirdly, and nevertheless, the
mention of 'external facts', as also the idea of emotion exceeding its
object, implies a separation of subject and object even as it recommends
a formula for overcoming that separation. It is sometimes claimed that
Eliot's use of the word 'external' is justified by the fact that he is
speaking here of a play, that the external is what is external to Hamlet's
mind but nevertheless internal to the play. This surely cannot meet the
case. For the passage explicitly generalizes about art and the artistic
process; and, to this extent consistently, it is ready to praise
Shakespeare's success elsewhere in these terms: 'you will find that the
state of mind of Lady Macbeth walking in her sleep has been communi-
cated to you by a skilful accumulation of imagined sensory
impressions'.[2] In other words, the success here lies not in any putative
adequacy to a represented situation in the play, but in that mode of
realization which, according to Eliot at this point, characterizes good
art: that is, the employment of sensory impressions. Nevertheless, it is
true that the whole passage is ambiguous as between the two senses of
'external facts; for when Eliot comes to speak of Hamlet's emotions
about his mother he is invoking the sense of a situation in the play. It is
not necessary in this context to delve into the difficulty which attends
this idea, though it might be indicated by what Eliot later says about
the reason why Shakespeare wrote *Hamlet*: 'we assume it to be an
experience which, in the manner indicated, exceeded the facts.'[3] If one
has an experience which 'exceeds the facts', is it illicit in art, or, for that
matter, in life? And since Eliot thinks that such experiences occur, why
cannot they constitute a kind of fact? Amidst the confusion and ambiguity one senses Eliot's partial adherence to an empiricist notion of art
and experience.

About the expression of emotion: in 'Tradition and the Individual

Talent' Eliot evolves a distinction between 'emotions' and 'feelings' which makes the latter the worthy form taken by emotion that is closely linked to its objects. The work of art 'may be formed out of one emotion, or may be a combination of several; and various feelings, inhering for the writer in particular words or phrases or images, may be added to compose the final result.'[4] Here emotion is a broad tonal wash, and feelings are closely bound up with the particular parts of the poem: they are emotion as involved in the objective correlative presented in art. A concentration on what Eliot terms 'emotions' may well lead to an inability to compose the 'numberless feelings, phrases, images' for which the poet's mind is a 'receptacle', into an adequate correlative. Eliot here writes out of a desire to add to the special status of the aesthetic experience, for which Pater and the late nineteenth century had prepared him, out of an almost formalist sense of how it is effected technically. Thus, while 'The effect of a work of art upon the person who enjoys it is an experience different in kind from any experience not of art', Eliot also wants to emphasize 'the intensity of the artistic process, the pressure, so to speak, under which the fusion takes place'.[5] Despite the influence of Flaubert and de Gourmont, Eliot's formulation is fresh and novel. Yet however he struggles with his distinction between emotion and feelings the basis of his theory remains affective.

As for the idea of a 'formula' this is another of those Modernist ruses for dressing up or disguising ideas of Romantic provenance in scientific terminology, as in the famous simile of filiated platinum from 'Tradition and the Individual Talent'. It can be compared to some of Pound's notions, though it also has an obvious source in Rémy de Gourmont's 'The Problem of Style': 'If, to the visual memory, the writer joins the emotive memory, and if he has the power, in evoking a material spectacle, of recovering the emotional state which that spectacle had aroused in him, then he possesses, even if he is ignorant, the whole art of writing.'[6] De Gourmont's description owes something to the Symbolist method. But he is also indebted to associationism, with that constant emphasis on sensations and physiology which led to his distrust of the 'dissociating intelligence', source of Eliot's 'dissociation of sensibility'.[7] He goes back to the English Empiricists for corroboration of his thoughts: 'Sensation is the basis of everything, of the moral and intellectual life as well as the physical life. Two hundred and fifty years after Hobbes, two hundred years after Locke, such has been the destructive power of religious Kantism that one is reduced to insisting on such elementary aphorisms.'[8] Wherever one looks in the modern period, even among Eliot's innovatory doctrines, one finds it hard to escape the universe first opened up by the early work of Wordsworth and Coleridge.

But the most interesting part of the passage on the 'objective correlative' is that which suggests a sharp separation of subject and object. For it implies that there is a basis in human psychology, even on Eliot's own terms, for art that expresses emotion in excess of its object. It may be bad art. But, in the nature of things, it is likely to occur. And further, one has to admit the possibility that Eliot is here warning the reader, and himself, against an affliction to which he himself felt vulnerable.

II

Hamlet, of course, also crops up in *Prufrock*: 'No! I am not Prince Hamlet, nor was meant to be.' The irony being that, however impotent Prufrock may feel, constantly disclaiming greatness ('I am no prophet – and here's no great matter') he does share one quality, at least, with the Prince: an inability to act:

> And time yet for a hundred indecisions,
> And for a hundred visions and revisions,
> Before the taking of a toast and tea . . .
>
> And indeed there will be time
> To wonder, 'Do I dare?' and, 'Do I dare?'
> Time to turn back and descend the stair . . .

Furthermore, it is not clear what the source of the indecision and shrinking from action is, unless it be, of course, a settled trait of Prufrock's character. And if this is what it is, it is still not clear what are the 'external facts' that have so painfully evinced this trait in the poem. Indeed, it makes a point of not being clear about this. What 'overwhelming question', for instance, is Prufrock trying to pop? The social situation – both the general context and the particular approach to a woman – give the air of a proposal of marriage. Yet the grave and portentous connotations invested in even so unlikely an event, as well as the paralysing difficulty of communication and definition, and not least the sense of being in Hell, all suggest a question about the transcendent. Both understandings of the nature of the question carry authority. And, as we shall see, it is entirely appropriate in an Eliot poem that despairing bafflement in the face of the transcendent should be conveyed in terms of discomfiture at the hands of a woman. But this general effect is overwhelmed by the mere sense of the indefinable:

> Would it have been worth while
> To have bitten off the matter with a smile
> To have squeezed the universe into a ball
> To roll it towards some overwhelming question,
> To say: 'I am Lazarus, come back from the dead,
> Come back to tell you all, I shall tell you all' –
> If one, settling a pillow by her head,
>   Should say: 'That is not what I meant at all.
>   That is not it, at all.'

The words about Lazarus, if they were spoken, would signify Prufrock's redemption from this seemingly petty circle of Hell. Such words are not spoken in Hell. But in any case, they are an assertion, not a question. And the woman's response, 'That is not what I meant', suggests an intangible situation where both are groping for appropriate words for what cannot be described. Prufrock himself is unable to articulate clear causes of his inaction: 'It is impossible to say just what I mean! / But as if a magic lantern threw the nerves in patterns on a screen.' Some settled pattern of his 'nerves', or character (fleetingly intuited) is to blame. Like the Hamlet Eliot describes, Prufrock 'is dominated by an emotion which is inexpressible, because it is in *excess* of the facts as they appear'.[9] The poem, like the play for Eliot, is 'full of some stuff that the writer could not drag to light, contemplate, or manipulate into art'.[10] As in *Hamlet*, this 'stuff' has to do with woman.

If Prufrock had even been capable of trying to redeem himself one feels that the woman would have rejected him. It is she who keeps him in Hell. Here she joins the other women of the poem, whose effect is to render him impotent and inarticulate:

> And I have known the eyes already, known them all –
> The eyes that fix you in a formulated phrase,
> And when I am formulated, sprawling on a pin,
> When I am pinned and wriggling on the wall,
> Then how should I begin
> To spit out all the butt-ends of my days and ways?

The women who 'come and go / Talking of Michelangelo' display a similar dangerous articulacy – an articulacy which is too confident of its efficacy, which believes too readily in the adequacy of words in a fallen world; for which facile force they are lampooned in the Michelangelo couplet.

And yet, by virtue of the very fact of ignoring fallenness, women, paradoxically, inhabit the confused, sensuous fallen world more confidently than men, or at least than Prufrock. They undermine his difficult efforts at formulation:

> And I have known the arms already, known them all –
> Arms that are braceleted and white and bare
> (But in the lamplight, downed with light brown hair!)
> Is it perfume from a dress
> That makes me so digress?

The sense of smell, which Eliot so often associates with women, sneaks around Prufrock's attempts at definition, and produces 'digression'. Yet the sensuousness of the women's arms is attractive, with a dangerous attractiveness which leads away from self-possession (women may erode this, as in 'Portrait of a Lady' (III)), away from the struggle with meaning. The one suggestion of Paradise afforded by the poem – the final vision of the mermaids – displays a similar ambivalence. For while it is 'human voices' (the language of the fallen world)[11] that 'wake us' so that 'we drown', the mermaids are seductive ancillary causes: 'We have lingered in the chambers of the sea / By sea-girls wreathed with seaweed red and brown / Till human voices wake us and we drown.' The 'stuff' that Eliot found hard to contemplate is the image of the *femme castratrice*, who eclipses even the view towards the transcendent. Unable to specify, but only to evoke, this 'stuff', he is left with 'no great matter' (the phrase is ambiguous). Prufrock cannot even bite off 'the matter'. Yet something about the poem's capaciousness (the range of modern urban scenes it contains) and about the narrator's knowingness (he knows something is rotten, even if he cannot say what) implies that this evocative treatment of 'no great matter' is intended to represent something important about the modern world. Just as Prufrock in some ways is Prince Hamlet, so he is from this point of view a prophet. The modern prophet has no great matter, and he knows it. In this way Eliot is already beginning to link sexual with spiritual sterility, individual and social, partly through the medium of a view of women that has elements of the pathological.

III

We saw above how the term 'objective correlative' is ambiguous. It may refer to 'external facts' (more problems there, which we have noted and now ignore); or to the author's presentation of a 'formula' for emotion. Even allowing for the treacherousness of the word 'external', 'Prufrock' lacks obvious candidates for the first sense. What about the second? Since one way of reading Eliot's critical passage is to see it as desiring a correlative to 'the facts', it might appear that the second could not exist without the first. But the passage is slightly confused, and it is certainly possible to see it as recommending simply a poetic method of presentment. It is this line that we shall pursue.

The question may seem easy to answer, and, in a sense, it is. Eliot does indeed present us with fragments possessing a relative tonal consistency with each other. Yet, once the clear 'external facts' are shown to be wanting, this answer becomes circular: does the poem provide a formula for its emotion? Yes. What is the emotion? The formula tells you. QED. In fact the only nugget of useful information imparted by the phrase 'objective correlative' is that Eliot uses an extreme Symbolist method of presenting items which together are intended to indicate a state of mind. The next question would be: what sort of items? The phrase might lead one to expect something to which the word 'objective' would in some way be appropriate. Eliot himself suggests 'a set of objects, a situation, a chain of events'. Yet what we get in 'Prufrock' is a medley of precise images, Laforguian or Tennysonian sonorities, Romantic lyricism, and ironic pastiche of Jacobean drama. Those imagistic parts do not sit at all ill with the others, for the whole poem works to convey to us that every part is subservient to the aim of representing a state of mind. The Prufrock persona is firmly in control of its utterances, despite its complexity. And we are not at all surprised by the extent to which statements or questions reflecting on the persona's putative state of mind dominate the poem, nor that they are so often cast in emotive form.

It is hard to avoid a conclusion such as this: Eliot as Symbolist; the phrase 'external facts' as even more pointless than usual; and the poetic 'formula' as part of a circular description of the Symbolist method. This conclusion holds good for a poem much closer in time to the 'Hamlet' essay: 'Gerontion'. Suppose one wished to claim pragmatic utility for the phrase 'external facts': one might claim that these are constituted by Gerontion's situation as an old man who has long lost faith and feeling, and, again, is incapable of action. But this does not add up to much. And there seems no point in denoting it, even for a moment, by that tricky word 'external'. In so far as a situation is alluded to, one may fancy it appears in these lines:

> I would meet you upon this honestly.
> I that was near your heart was removed therefrom
> To lose beauty in terror, terror in inquisition.
> I have lost my passion: why should I need to keep it
> Since what is kept must be adulterated?
> I have lost my sight, smell, hearing, taste and touch:
> How should I use them for your closer contact?

These lines certainly evoke the idea of an estranged beloved. Yet there are sufficient hints at loss of religious faith for us to be unsure: '"We would see a sign!"'; 'The word within a word'; 'Christ the tiger'; references to the Mass. Perhaps 'you' represents Christ, then. In fact 'you' is better thought of as a lyric 'other', comprising both erotic and religious connotations. But this only ties us back to the emphasis on the speaker's represented state of mind.

Of course, with Hugh Kenner, one may see Eliot as attempting to

nudge the reader into a kind of meta-view of the relation between the
speaker's condition and his rhetoric.[12] Eliot may have been applying his
own descriptions of Senecan stoicism and its influence on Elizabethan
drama: 'the ethic of Seneca's plays is that of an age which supplied the
lack of moral habits by a system of attitudes and poses'; 'Stoicism is
the refuge for the individual in an indifferent or hostile world too big
for him; it is the permanent substratum of a number of versions of
cheering oneself up . . . The stoical attitude is the reverse of Christian
humility.'[13] This stratagem – and Kenner's argument is persuasive – is
an interesting twist in the Browning tradition of the ironic dramatic
monologue. But it does not affect our understanding of the poem as
Symbolist in a way that cannot be made to square with Eliot's attempt,
in his theory of the 'objective correlative', to provide some external
measure against which the kind and quantity of emotion could be
judged. It is instructive to note that Eliot describes Senecan rhetoric in
terms that suggest that very excess of emotion over its object he
castigates in *Hamlet*: 'the tendency to "rhetoric" . . . which on such a
large scale, may be attributed to a development of language exceeding
the development of sensibility of the people.'[14] So far, then, we have
concluded, by taking a different route, in agreeing with Donald Davie
that Eliot is a Symbolist poet.[15] But on the way we have raised questions
about the status of the 'objective', the image of woman, and the use of
language. These become more pressing and complex in relation to *The
Waste Land*.

IV

Nobody needs reminding that *The Waste Land* is a fragmentary poem.
What is sometimes less well understood is the fact that Eliot did not
even have a unified poem in mind at the time of writing the fragments,
as the genesis of 'The Waste Land MSS' makes clear.[16] A unifying strand
is provided by the theme of spiritual sterility, which is underpinned by
references to vegetative myths, and especially to that of the Fisher King,
impotent ruler of an infertile land and people. This figure is described in
Jessie L. Weston's *From Ritual to Romance*, to which Eliot refers in his

notes to the poem, and she relates it to the figure of King Pelleas in the Grail legend. Closely linked to the theme of sterility is the familiar tale of inaction and inarticulacy in the presence of woman. Near the beginning of the poem, the fragment on the hyacinth girl seems to offer a moment of insight into love:

> – Yet when we came back late, from the hyacinth garden,
> Your arms full, and your hair wet, I could not
> Speak, and my eyes failed, I was neither
> Living nor dead, and I knew nothing
> Looking into the heart of light, the silence.

But such positive weight as this carries is undermined by the next line, from *Tristan und Isolde*, *'Oed' und leer das Meer'*, 'Desolate and empty the sea', which in context implies that the failure to speak is cause of loss of love.

The end of the poem raises the theme of inaction in memorable from:

> What have we given?
> My friend, blood shaking my heart
> The awful daring of a moment's surrender
> Which an age of prudence can never retract . . .

> The boat responded
> Gaily, to the hand expert with sail and oar
> The sea was calm, your heart would have responded
> Gaily, when invited, beating obedient
> To controlling hands

This topic, as in 'Prufrock', underscores the fact that *The Waste Land* represents an isolated, disconnected state of mind, summed up in lines from the same passage:

> I have heard the key
> Turn in the door and turn once only
> We think of the key, each in his prison
> Thinking of the key, each confirms a prison
> Only at nightfall, aetherial rumours
> Revive for a moment a broken Coriolanus

The solipsism is inescapable. Eliot glosses this passage in his notes with a quotation from Bradley's *Appearance and Reality*:

> My external sensations are no less private to my self than are my thoughts and feelings. In either case my experience falls within my own circle, a circle closed on the outside; and, with all its elements alike, every sphere is opaque to the others which surround it ... In brief, regarded as an existence which appears in a soul, the whole world for each is peculiar and private to that soul.

There is complexity here, for Bradley rejected the idea that his philosophy was solipsistic. That notion would only be true, he argued, if the Self were given in Immediate Experience, which is Bradley's starting point, and which he thinks of as the starting point for individual. But, Bradley claimed, the Self is a construct which is gradually derived from experience. And Eliot agreed with him on this point.[17] These facts serve only to show that Eliot's poetic feeling for isolation was more powerful than a fine philosophical distinction. Yet the passage from Bradley is illuminating about the whole poem, and not only these few lines. The phrase, 'My external sensations are no less private to my self than are my thoughts and feelings' has some points in common with the circular definition of the successful poem: a text where sensations, thoughts and feelings are presented together and add up to a state of mind. *The Waste Land* takes this definition further than 'Prufrock' and 'Gerontion' in terms of fragmentariness: the heterogeneity of registers and experiences it encompasses. But the intention is the same.

It is not surprising, then, that Eliot should attempt to provide that poem not just with the unity of myth, but also with a unifying *persona*. Tiresias is 'the most important personage in the poem, uniting all the rest', the notes declare. There is a danger of taking this too seriously. Of course, Eliot is attracted by any notion which might confer some kind of unity on 'these fragments', and it is futile to deny that he would probably have seen Tiresias' hermaphroditism as 'analogous to the castration of the Fisher King';[18] or that Tiresias' bisexuality, prophetic powers and aged wisdom made him seem an appropriate figure to record the inclusive feeling of disillusionment which pervades the poem. Yet, unlike Prufrock and Gerontion, Tiresias is not provided with a consistent attempt at the representation of a voice. And the reader can only get him working in the poem for any length of time by a constant reference back to Eliot's *ex post facto* assertion.

Better, perhaps, to enquire more closely why Tiresias should assume such importance for Eliot. The myth, which is conveyed by a long quotation from Ovid in his notes, is that Tiresias came across two snakes copulating in a forest. When he hit them with his staff he was turned into a woman. Seven years later, when he again came across two snakes, he hit them again – perhaps understandably thinking this would do the trick in reverse. It did. Because of the experience thus gained he was called in by Jove to adjudicate in a quarrel he was having with Juno. Jove claimed that women enjoy greater sexual pleasure than men. Juno argued the contrary. Tiresias supported Jove and, out of spite, Juno struck him blind. In recompense, Jove gave Tiresias the power of prophecy and the gift of longevity. The bare facts of this account convey a certain misogyny: the castrating force of female sexuality; the superior and intellectual gift of prophecy conferred by Jove. But Eliot's interest in the myth should be seen in the light of Freud.

From the point of view of Freud's hypothesis of the Oedipus complex, Tiresias' initial sighting of two snakes copulating suggests the primal scene (the child's conception of its parents copulating). The conversion of the parents into snakes would be a phantasy in which the repressed Oedipal knowledge of the prime value attached to the father's possession of the phallus expresses itself in disguised form: it is snakes that copulate. Similarly, Tiresias' transformation into a woman expresses in disguised form the fear of castration that such knowledge brings. His subsequent return to his original sex represents the acceptance of the father's possession of the phallus. The second part of the story, concerning Jove and Juno, gives further symbols of the father and mother. Tiresias' assertion that women enjoy greater sexual pleasure than men again accords primacy to possession of the phallus: it is the more pleasurable object. Juno's act in blinding him symbolizes the way in which the child's recognition of the mother's desire may serve as a confirmation of the threat of castration. In some circumstances the child may become fixated on this image of the mother. Other facts about Tiresias lend confirmation to the idea that Eliot apprehended the story at some level in these terms. The most famous 'scene' the legendary Tiresias 'perceived' was the story of Oedipus itself. Oedipus' incest caused Thebes to become an infertile waste land, under a curse like the other afflicted lands to which Eliot's poem alludes. Since Tiresias is supposed to be 'the most important personage in the poem, uniting all the rest', having 'foresuffered all', it is reasonable to feel that the Oedipus story is the most important allusion in the poem – perhaps none the less for being unmentioned.

Freud certainly indicates the way in which aspects of the Oedipal triangle may manifest themselves in 'abnormal' ways in the adult life of males. Thus, in 'A Special Type of Choice of Object Made by Men', he considers the cases of men who always prefer women to be attached, married or of bad sexual repute.[19] In these cases the man is compelled to repeat the situation in which the mother's first desire is for the father. The case of *Hamlet*, on the other hand, shows Shakespeare, according to Freud, translating his own revived feelings about his parents on the death of his father in 1601.[20] Hamlet finds it hard to take vengeance on 'the man who did away with his father and took that father's place with his mother, the man who shows him the repressed wishes of his own childhood realised'.[21] His 'distaste for sexuality' accords with his unconscious recognition of his own desire for his mother.[22] It also accords with the confirmation of the threat of castration provided by the mother's desire for the father. This complex image of the mother lies behind Eliot's presentation of women, and explains his fascinated difficulty with *Hamlet*. Perhaps it is worth noting that Eliot's own father died in 1919, shortly before the composition of the Hamlet essay, and that this was a 'terrible ordeal for him'.[23]

The treatment of sexuality and of women in *The Waste Land* tends to confirm the view outlined here. Women may be the source of a tired, meaningless, sterile sexuality: the woman with the 'synthetic perfumes' in 'A Game of Chess'; the cockney proponent of abortion for Lil, in the same section; the typist in 'The Fire Sermon'; even Elizabeth I. This undervaluing of women's sexuality is one way of coping with the Oedipal problem that the mother's desire is not for oneself. Even Eliot's idealized hyacinth girl can be accommodated in the picture, since the kind of pathology described here includes the idealization of women who conform to the image of the mother in her proper role of 'good' woman. But strictly speaking, the hyacinth girl, like Ophelia, is a kind of middle case, evoking an ambivalent reaction.

It is woman who 'confuses the sense' in Eliot and renders impossible the ideal fusion of word and thing or word and thought, attainable in the Bradleyan Absolute.[24] Eliot is left in a Hell where there is nothing to link the items which occur to the isolated consciousness except the very myth of woman's destruction of meaning itself. For although *The Waste Land* attempts to point up the contrast between past and present in a way that stresses the squalor of the latter in mock-heroic fashion, this ruse is undercut by the implication that fallen sexuality is a universal feature of human society: Elizabeth and Leicester may not have 'oil and tar' to contend with, but they are still corrupt; Tiresias may observe the typist and the young man carbuncular with distaste, but it is a distaste that he has foresuffered. The past comes to *stand in* for an ideal, for the ideal cannot be realized in history. In this way the isolated modern consciousness, striving to find meaning in a world deprived of agreed myths, consorts with a particular pathology and comes to fasten on the myth of a fallen sexuality, deriving from woman, both as the condition and the cause of fallenness.

But if woman destroys man's ability to create the full, phallic word, what are the specific effects of this on language? Partly the Babel of registers in early Eliot; partly the fragmentariness of construction; but also partly the continued dependence on suggestive, emotive language. Like Pound, Eliot did not think he could get through Hell in a hurry. The formula of the objective correlative is partly intended to save the emotive aspect of Eliot's technique from the aspersion of 'Romantic' expressivism: passionate cries and imprecise sonorities become objects or data in the poet's experience, on an equal footing with exact perception and witty intellection. Yet in fact they bear witness to the continued power of the Romantic and post-Romantic tradition over Eliot's practice.

And this may be no bad thing. What Eliot can still offer us is the model of a Modernist poetry ready to experiment with *montage* techniques and the clash of registers, but free from the constricting effects of a more complete submission to empiricist ways of thinking about the place of language in poetry. In this way, like Pound (but unlike many of Pound's axioms) he has perhaps more to offer a postmodern poetry than some of his immediate successors.

4

WILLIAM CARLOS WILLIAMS

I

'No ideas but in things.' The phrase from *Paterson* I is well known, and although Yvor Winters is right to see it as, 'like Pound's imagism . . . an end-product of eighteenth-century associationism',[1] it is for this very reason that it seems like the merest 'common sense' to many, including literary critics.[2] Winters's remark is very general, and not very informative for the reader who does not know Williams. And it may be quite misleading for a European unaware of the pragmatist revision of empiricism brought about in the work of William James and John Dewey. Yet a closer glance at Williams's work reveals that, in so far as he holds an identifiable view on the relationship between the mind and the senses, it does not seem much different from the way in which some Romantics conceived it. His originality lies, as with Pound and other Modernists, in the radical formal methods he deduces from post-Romantic postulates, and a tendency to stress broadly empiricist elements, within the complex position he adopts, in a radical and provocative manner.

The sort of statement one finds in the prose parts of *Spring and All* is often repeated:

> Imagination is wrongly understood when it is supposed to be a removal from reality in the sense of John of Gaunt's speech in Richard the Second: to imagine possession of that which is lost. It is rightly understood when John of Gaunt's words are related not to their sense as objects adherent to

his son's welfare or otherwise but as a dance over the body of his condition accurately accompanying it.

The insistence on reality is characteristic and familiar. But there is an ambiguity about this and other such statements in *Spring and All*: the use of the word 'imagination'; the idea of words as a 'dance over' their object – typically balanced, however, by that 'accurately'. Williams is not always so troubled by the relationship of subject and object. Or at least, not troubled enough to engage in the delicate balancing act he constantly attempts in *Spring and All*. Thus in *Paterson* one finds the poet intends 'To make a start / out of particulars / and make them general' asserting the classic empiricist view of the relationship between the general and the particular, and of the mode of acquiring knowledge.[4] Elsewhere we are reminded that there are 'No ideas but / in the facts' and that there are 'accuracies' of 'events' that 'surpass' language.[5] It would be tedious to enumerate the many examples of such thinking in Williams, examples which link him, like Pound, back to Emerson and Thoreau ('The roots of letters are things') and thus finally to what I have called the universe opened up by Wordsworth and Coleridge. But there are also many examples of a more hesitant approach to these matters. The struggle with the relationship of subject and object begins in earnest in *Kora in Hell*, where the emphasis is more on 'imagination' than on the 'thing': 'The imagination transcends the thing itself.'[6] Some of these formulations are, in fact, very similar to those of *Spring and All:* '*The wish would be to see not floating visions of unknown purport but the imaginative qualities of the actual things being perceived accompany their gross vision in a slow dance, interpreting as they go.*'[7] But here, unlike in *Spring and All*, we are permitted to be totally subjective if we have to be, for this ideal relationship is not always possible: the passage ends, '*But inasmuch as this will not always be the case one must dance nevertheless as he can.*' Still, there are doubts about the admissibility of this; these are allegorized in the second improvisation in Section **XXV**:

A man can shoot his spirit up out of a wooden house, that is, through the roof – the roof's slate – but how far? It is of final importance to know that. To say the world turns under my feet and that I watch it passing with a smile is neither the truth nor my desire. But I would wish to stand

– you've seen the kingfisher do it – where the largest town might be taken in my two hands, as high let us say as a man's head – some one man not too far above the clouds.[8]

The 'interpretation' of this improvised effusion is, as always, appended in italics: *'It is obvious that if in flying an airplane one reached such an altitude that all sense of direction and every intelligible perception of the world were lost there would be nothing left to do but to come down to that point at which eyes regained their power.'*[9] Near the end of *Kora in Hell*, in Section XXVII, we are offered a more exact formula which points the way forward to the more obviously Cubist-influenced poetics of *Spring and All*:

> The particular thing, whether it be four pinches of four divers white powders cleverly compounded to cure surely, safely, pleasantly a painful twitching of the eyelids or say a pencil sharpened at one end, dwarfs the imagination, makes logic a butterfly, offers a finality that sends us spinning through space, a fixity the mind could climb forever, a revolving mountain, as complexity with a surface of glass; the gist of poetry. *D. C. al fin.*[10]

Here the 'fixity' and 'finality' of the object are unaffected by the imagination, whose role is to explore its aspects in a manner akin to the cubist analysis of planes and their relations.

In *Spring and All* there are constant efforts to describe a relationship between subject and object where the latter is unaffected by human perception but may nevertheless seem different in imagination: art has to convey both facts: the impenetrability of objects and their imaginative transformation – a difficult notion:

> Imagination is not to avoid reality, nor is it description nor an evocation of objects or situations, it is to say that poetry does not tamper with the world but moves it – It affirms reality most powerfully and therefore, since reality needs no personal support but exists free from human action, as proven by science in the indestructibility of matter and force, it creates a new object, a play, a dance which is not a mirror up to nature but –
>
> As birds' wings beat the solid air without which none could fly so words freed by the imagination affirm reality by their flight.[11]

Yet again we have the oft-repeated notion of the poet's words as dancing next to reality, and not too far away from it either. The same idea occurs in *Paterson*: 'The vague accuracies of events dancing two and two with language which they forever surpass'.[12] But beyond the fact that objects must be allowed their objective status, while imagination 'moves' but does not 'tamper' with them, it is hard to be more specific. Williams wants, like many Modernists, to play up an empiricism he thinks of as anti-Romantic. But he wants to speak of the transforming imagination with all the old reverence at the same time. The definitions in *Spring and All* slop back and forth between 'imagination' and 'reality', but never close the gap far enough to show the precise nature of the encounter. In this regard, the only advantage Williams acquires over Romantic discourse is that he does not attempt precise definitions he cannot sustain. Indeed, in *Paterson* he concedes that 'nothing is so unclear, between man and his writing, as to which is the man and which the thing and of them both which is the more to be valued'.[13] In *I Wanted to Write a Poem* he says of the prose passages in *Spring and All*: 'The prose is a mixture of philosophy and nonsense. It made sense to me, at least to my disturbed mind – because it *was* disturbed at that time – but I doubt if it made sense to anyone else.'[14] He is a little unfair to himself. But the remark reveals an understandable feeling that he had failed to be more than suggestive. But whatever suggestive – or even nonsensical – qualifications are made, the world of things is simply and inalienably there. 'This naive realism,' as Hugh Kenner says, 'through which any philosopher would promptly drive a Mack truck, sufficed, for Williams, to free the poet from anxieties he hadn't the patience for.'[15] Critics have been ready to follow his lead. A. D. Moody, speaking of Wordsworth's objectivity, goes on to say: 'The mainstream of poetry in English has advanced on Wordsworth by cultivating a further degree of objectivity, to the extent of seeking to identify the mind wholly with its object. There is an instance near the beginning of . . . *Paterson*, where the mind observing the Passaic Falls becomes them for a moment.'[16] These remarks betray no trace of philosophical anxiety, although, admittedly, this point would scarcely be worth making if it were not for the way it illustrates the easy acceptance enjoyed by naive realism.

The side of Williams that feels the imperturbability of things goes to photography rather than Cubism, and is attracted by the 'creed' of Americanism, photography and the 'object', described by Ruth Grogan:

the creed advocates a reconciliation between the American artist and his own environment, a doctrine which merges with the conviction that the 'self' can only be discovered by fidelity to the objective world; the outer world is full of forms awaiting discovery, and these forms, if faithfully responded to, express and reveal the inner truth of the 'I'. These premises sprout easily into, on the one hand a primitivistic myth of the soil and sexuality, and on the other hand, a challenge to adapt to the modern urban and industrial environment. [17]

The other side of Williams, the one that stresses imagination, is happy to repeat the most vaunting themes of Romantic discourse. There is, for instance, 'a man of imagination' who struggles with 'demoded words' which have lost their 'vitality' – a vitality he feels within himself. [18] By means of imagination the poet comes to feel that he is as large as the universe (the return of the sublime) and possesses a kinship with it:

> The inevitable flux of the seeing eye toward measuring itself by the world it inhabits can only result in *himself* crushing humiliation unless the individual raise to some approximate co-extension with the universe. This is possible by the aid of the imagination. Only through the agency of this force can a man feel himself moved largely with sympathetic pulses at work _ [19]

One might sum up Williams's view of the poet and objects in this way: the poet confronts a world of things and attempts to render them with impeccable accuracy, but nevertheless according to a fresh, imaginative ordering. The precise terms of the relationship are left unclear. But the fact that the enterprise occurs at all is a result of a vitality in the poet that recognizes a kindred vitality in the universe.

II

Williams's ideas about language assume that it is merely a transparent medium for registering items in a transaction between poet and reality, as in Pound's Imagist formulations. And there are the same ambiguities about the extent to which the poet's subjectivity is registered, ambiguities which reflect the ambiguous epistemology of both poets.

Certainly, like Pound, Williams often speaks as if language is properly
a pale reflection of things. Events 'surpass' language. This notion is
allegorized in the description 'Earth, the chatterer, father of all /
speech'.[20] But another emphasis is there too, one that sees language as
reflecting the encounter of imagination with things. In *Spring and All*
the 'man of imagination' has to contend with words that have become
'demoded' and lacking in 'vitality' 'because meanings have been lost
through laziness or changes in the form of existence'.[21] There is a whole
area of language which is dead and deadening because it has come adrift
from the thing, or from experience, depending on the version at hand.
This is the area of cliché, of penumbral meaning and inflated rhetoric.
One must return to unsullied reference, of which the emblem, in
Paterson, is the River Passaic:

> Quit it. Quit this place. Go where all
> mouths are rinsed: to the river for
> an answer
>   for relief from 'meaning'[22]

There is no sense of society's participation in the creation of meanings,
no sense of language as conveying that participation. The social, the
political, appear as filthy and corrupting agencies:

> A voice calling in the hubbub (Why else
> are there newspapers, by the cart-load?) blaring
> the news no wit shall evade, no rhyme
> cover. Necessity gripping the words   .   scouting
> evasion, that love is begrimed, befouled[23]

Not only the present, but also the diachronic form of the social
– tradition – may threaten the purity of the living word: especially
literary tradition, words from the past. A whole section of *Paterson* (Book
Three, 'The Library') revolves around the idea of burning books: barren
leaves, indeed. And although this notion is ambiguous, connoting both
the destruction of dead verbiage and the word flaming thereby with new
life, the iconoclastic element is quite salient, and implies a violent
rejection of the social determination of meanings. What Williams would
see as society's contribution to meaning is viewed as an historical

deposit, acquired rather than natural, burying the pure stream of experience.

The idea of a stream of experience – symbolized in *Paterson* by the Passaic River – should serve to recall the revisions of empiricism undertaken in the work of the American philosophers William James and John Dewey; their beliefs must be seen as influencing Williams's cultural background. Especially noteworthy is James's refusal to subscribe to the doctrine – characteristic of the British empiricist tradition – that *connections* between sense-data are not part of experience, but rather impositions of the mind on singular discrete impressions. James's 'radical empiricism' involved a return, as he saw it, to the purity of immediate experience, conceived as what he called an 'activity situation', but free of socially determined preconception. As such it is very reminiscent of Husserl's 'phenomenological reduction'. Another doctrine of classic empiricism rejected by James was that of the passivity of the mind in experience: rather, it was to be seen as always interested, purposeful, willing. Williams's lucubrations about the relationship of imagination and object have to be seen as part of a specifically American ambience, as does the refreshing emphasis on process which is to be found in his poems.

In creating the living word the poet also revives the line of poetry according to a new measure:

> without invention the line
> will never again take on its ancient
> divisions when the word, a supple word,
> lived in it, crumbled now to chalk.[24]

This is the Romantic paradox of the original genius who merely recovers an ancient vision, an ancient union of word and experience. The new measure is seen in one aspect as a precise organic fit with the 'objective' world: 'Measure is the only solidity we are permitted to know in our sensible world, to measure.'[25] Or, in a notably empiricist version: 'The first thing you learn when you begin to learn anything about this earth is that you are eternally barred save for the report of your senses from knowing anything about it. Measure serves for us as the key: we can measure between objects; therefore, we know that they exist.'[26] But this view represents only a momentary emphasis on one side of the recurrent object – subject couple. At the same time we find Williams laying the stress on the expressive vitality of the speaker, as in this metaphor of dance: 'Poetry began with measure, it began with the dance, whose divisions we have all but forgotten, but are still known as measures. Measures they were and we still speak of their minuter elements as feet.'[27] Yet again the ambiguity: as in Romanticism, the organic metaphor is applied both to the poetic treatment of things, and to the energy of the poet. The latter emphasis also issues in Williams's famous desire to capture the rhythm and intonation of American speech – 'the very language of men' in America: for the rootedness of a particular form of speech is one guarantee of its organically spontaneous nature.

The organic metaphor spills over into tides and ripples in Williams's 1913 essay on 'English Speech Rhythms':

> Imagination creates an image, piece by piece, segment by segment – into a whole, living. But each part as it plays into its neighbor, each segment into its neighbor segment and every part into every other, causing the whole – exists naturally in rhythm, and as there are waves there are tides and as there are ridges in the sand there are bars after bars . . .
>
> Each piece of work, rhythmic in whole, is then in essence an assembly of tides, waves, ripples – in short, of greater and lesser rhythmic particles regularly repeated or destroyed.[28]

But even at the end of this passage there is a covert reference to the wave/particle duality in the description of light. As so often in Modernism, especially in America, the boundaries between organicist metaphor and scientific description are eroded. Not surprisingly, then, organic waves may easily become mechanical ones:

> A poem is a small (or large) machine made of words. When I say there's nothing sentimental about a poem I mean that there can be no part, as in any other machine, that is redundant.
>
> Prose may carry a load of ill-defined matter like a ship. But poetry is the machine which drives it, pruned to a perfect economy. As in all machines its movement is intrinsic, undulant, a physical more than a literary character.[29]

Williams's invention of 'the variable foot' is an extreme organicist conception of the uses of rhythm, embodied in language that indicates an indebtedness to science, in the form of popularized versions of the theory of relativity:[30]

> My dissatisfaction with free verse came to a head in that I always wanted a verse that was ordered, so it came to me that the concept of the foot itself would have to be altered in our new relativistic world . . . The foot not being fixed is only to be described as variable. If the foot itself is variable it allows order in so-called free verse. Thus the verse becomes not free at all but just variable, as all things in life properly are.[31]

He gives an example of the kind of thing he has in mind in a letter to Richard Eberhart (23 May 1954):

count: – not that I ever count when writing but, at best the lines must
         be capable of being counted, that is to say, *measured* . . .
(approximate example)

      (1) The smell of the heat is boxwood
         (2)   when rousing us
            (3)   a movement of the air
    (4)   stirs our thoughts
       (5)   that had no life in them
         (6)   to a life, a life in which
    . . .

Count a single beat to each numeral.[32]

The 'variable foot', then, is defined by the fact that the poet intends us to read each line as counting a heavy stress, however few or many be the syllables. This is one of those ideas that may seem to make obvious sense to readers who want to accept a modernized version of organicism. But the theory is vague, and the practice does not support it. Not that it really matters whether or not Williams has succeeded in elaborating a coherent theory. Much of his verse carries great rhythmic conviction in any case. Yet paradoxically the incoherence can serve to highlight the genuinely original aspects of his verse in clearer terms. And a consideration of his versification may also provide a convenient way into the texture of his poems themselves.

III

From early on Williams would have no truck with the idea of total freedom in verse: even in 1917 he could explain: '"free verse" is a misnomer'; verse 'must be governed'.[33] And such was to remain his point of view. Taking this with what he says about measure and the variable foot, there seems no reason to doubt that he had in mind a relative regularity in the distribution of stresses. Sometimes the regularity can be quite marked:

> The decay of cathedrals
> is efflorescent
> through the phenomenal
> growth of movie houses
>
> whose catholicity is
> progress since
> destruction and creation
> are simultaneous[34]

Arguably these are all two-beat lines, and furthermore all but one have unstressed endings, with either one or two unstressed syllables. A good example of a markedly two-beat poem occurs in the same volume:

> The veritable night
> of wires and stars
>
> the moon is in
> the oak tree's crotch
>
> and sleepers in
> the windows cough
>
> athwart the round
> and pointed leaves

> and insects sting
> while on the grass
>
> the whitish moonlight
> tearfully
>
> assumes the attitudes
> of afternoon — [35]

Here the iamb itself struts rather than lurks. But elsewhere the measure is not so easy to describe:

> As the cát
> climbed óver
> the tóp of
>
> the jám closet
> fírst the right
> fórefoot
>
> cárefully
> then the hínd
> stepped dówn
>
> into the pít of
> the émpty
> flówerpot
>
> ('Poem')

I have added a plausible 'speech rhythm' distribution of heavy stresses. Two things are clear: first that the tendency to two-beat rhythmic units is present again; but secondly that these units do not correspond to the line divisions. A similar incommensurability tends to obtain even after Williams has invented the term 'variable foot'. Indeed, it is worth looking at the passage he himself quotes in *I Wanted to Write a Poem* as one which helped him to formulate the idea[36]:

> The descént beckons
>   as the ascént beckoned
>   Mémory is a kind
> of accómplishment

a sórt of renéwal
       éven
an initiátion, since the spáces it opens are néw
pláces
       inhábited by hórdes
              héretofore unréalized
of néw kínds –
    since their móvements
       are towards néw objéctives
(even though fórmerly they were abándoned)

No deféat is made up entírely of defeat – since
the wórld it opens is always a pláce
    fórmerly
       unsuspécted. A
wórld lóst,
    a wórld unsuspécted
       béckons to new pláces
and no whíteness (lost) is so whíte as the mémory
of whíteness

Again I have added a plausible score for the heavy stresses. But there are
other ways of seeing the pattern, and this does not allow for the
importance of 'middle-weight' beats. In any case, there is no way of
making the line divisions conform to any conceivable pattern of stresses,
even though there is a tendency to rhythmic pattern that ignores
lineation: yet again the tendency is to two-beat units, which are cut
across by the lineation, rather than being set into it. An interesting, and
simpler, example comes from an earlier period:

              the unused tent
              of

              bare beams
              beyond which

              directly wait
              the night

              and day –
              Here

from the street
by

        * * *
        * S *
        * O *
        * D *
        * A *
        * * *

ringed with
running lights

the darkened
pane

exactly
down the center

is
transfixed

('The Attic which is Desire')

Yet again a predominantly two-beat pattern is cut across by the lineation. And the representational typographic effect of the printing of
'SODA' may serve as a reminder of the conscious way in which Williams
experimented with the look of the words on the page; the experiment
included the arrangement of lines. When Jonathan Culler quotes the
poem 'This is Just to Say' to show how the special reading attention
required for poetry may be mustered simply by the arrangement into
lines of what would otherwise be a banal message, he is doing more than
shedding light on the reading of poems:[37]

I have eaten
the plums
that were in
the icebox

and which
you were probably
saving

for breakfast

Forgive me
they were delicious
so sweet
and so cold

Culler is also shedding light on something fundamental to Williams's verse. For this is indeed a poem that exists to do exactly what Culler says. It does not use typographical placing in a particularly interesting way. There is little charge imparted by the fact that a slight delay is enacted between 'eaten' and 'the plums', or 'saving' and 'for breakfast'. No: this is an almost pure exercise in what typography can do to make a poem – almost, because there is also a pattern of four stresses per stanza and one per line. Yet Williams frequently does more than this, exploiting the slight suspense that may be enacted by line-endings, as in 'Young Woman at a Window', for instance:

She sits with
tears on

her cheek
her cheek on

her hand
the child

in her lap
his nose

pressed
to the glass

In this, as in many another poem, typography works with the ideal of objectivity to create a careful attention to each fact and to the relationships between them. This is often Williams's way of finding food for the imagination in the mundane.

The relatively 'mechanical' device of careful typographical disposition runs counter to the largely organicist implications of the idea of measure as Williams expresses it. This is partly in the nature of things: typography and voice cannot be converted into each other except in terms of vague and equivocal approximation. How do you read out an indentation? How do you signal its difference from an ordinary line break? The more ambitious and complex the typographical effects, the more obvious it is that they belong irreducibly to a different order from that of phonic effects. But two points must be made: first, that there is no reason, apart from a mystical attachment to voice as the essence of poetry, why poets should not use typography; and secondly, that it may be rewarding to exploit the interplay of typographic and phonic effects, though this means that the text must be available to the eye. The second reason for the contradiction in Williams's practice is, as we have seen, that he often disposes his lineation in a pattern that does not conform to that of the stresses. So while one need not take too seriously the 'mechanical' dress Williams gives to organic speech rhythms (except to note his need to do so), it really is true that his typographic effects are anti-organicist in the sense that they cut across the dispositions of words that might be generated by rhythmic units, and suggest another ordering based on cool and careful reflection. The result – a counterpoint for eye and breath – derives from a characteristically American amalgam of the vital and the mechanical in Williams's thinking. To demystify Williams's poetics is not to reject them. On the contrary, cut away from their tangled theoretical moorings, and from the quasi-empiricist ideology which accompanies them, they can be seen to provide for a flexible rhythmic verse, fruitfully complicated and enriched by a typographic ordering which escapes the reduction of the poem to the poet's voice.

IV

For Williams, as for Pound, questions of gender are closely related to those of poetics. His metaphorical use of the idea of woman can be seen writ large in the Blakean giant Paterson, who is both a city and a man:

A man like a city and a woman like a flower
– who are in love. Two women. Three women.

> Innumerable women, each like a flower.
>
>   But
> only one man − like a city.[38]

The male sex is representative of humanity. Woman remains at the level of the particular: a compliment, of course, from a poet who prizes particularity. As he had already written many years before, 'Man is the vague generalizer, woman the concrete thinker, and not the reverse as he imagined.'[39] This remark does not allow for the reversibility of most gender stereotypes: in the inventory of these, woman the concrete thinker is surely as common as woman the vague and emotional. In any case, it remains a back-handed compliment, for the aim of the poet, as expressed at the beginning of *Paterson* I, is:

> To make a start
> out of particulars
> and make them general, rolling
> up the sum . . .[40]

The superiority of the male poet, implied, though not stated, in this and other places, is that he can properly register particulars while at the same time being able to make valid generalizations from them: a sensitive and an intellectual being.

In the lines about the city, woman is also 'like a flower': the particularizing consciousness of women is organic, unreflective and receptive. These associations are reinforced by other passages in *Paterson*. Thus, in so far as woman can be seen in general terms, it is as the mountain, stretched out beside the masculine city, with the Park (no doubt full of flowers) at 'her' head: 'And there, against him, stretches the low mountain. / The Park's her head, curved, above the Falls, by the quiet / river'.[41] Both the association with the particular and that with organism are linked and explained in Williams's letter to *The Egoist*, commenting on the contributions of Dora Marsden concerning sexual psychology:

> I think it is fairly safe to say that male psychology is characterized by an inability to concede reality to fact. This has arisen no doubt from the

universal lack of attachment between the male and an objective world –
to the earth under feet – since the male, aside from his extremely simple
sex function, is wholly unnecessary to objective life: the only life which
his sense perceives. He can never be even certain that his child is his own.
From this may arise some of the feeling a man has for his mother, for in
her at least is a connexion with the earth, if only a passive one.[42]

Williams sees his espousal of the objective in art as the renewal of lost
psychic harmony through the rediscovery of a feminine mode of consciousness. Yet the harmony always transcends the feminine alone. This
can be seen very clearly in *Paterson*, but it is also implicit in the
confident, generalizing discursiveness of many an earlier poem, as one
can see when one knows what the gender associations of such a mode
were for Williams. His attitude can most clearly be gauged from some
of the poems where he treats of women. For a patronizing note often
intrudes, deriving from that very association of woman with the natural
that was meant to constitute her superiority. That fine poem from *Spring
and All*, XVIII, 'The pure products of America', later entitled 'For
Elsie', is a good example:

> The pure products of America
> go crazy –
> mountain folk from Kentucky
>
> or the ribbed north end of
> Jersey
> with its isolate lakes and
>
> valleys, its deaf-mutes, thieves
> old names
> and promiscuity between
>
> devil-may-care men who have taken
> to railroading
> out of sheer lust of adventure –
>
> and young slatterns, bathed
> in filth
> from Monday to Saturday
>
> to be tricked out that night

with gauds
from imaginations which have no

peasant traditions to give them
character
but flutter and flaunt

sheer rags — succumbing without
emotion
save numbed terror

under some hedge of choke-cherry
or viburnum —
which they cannot express —

Unless it be that marriage
perhaps
with a dash of Indian blood

will throw up a girl so desolate
so hemmed round
with disease or murder

that she'll be rescued by an
agent —
reared by the state and

sent out at fifteen to work in
some hard-pressed
house in the suburbs —

some doctor's family, some Elsie —
voluptuous water
expressing with broken

brain the truth about us —
her great
ungainly hips and flopping breasts

addressed to cheap
jewelry
and rich young men with fine eyes

as if the earth under our feet
were

an excrement of some sky

and we degraded prisoners
destined
to hunger until we eat filth

while the imagination strains
after deer
going by fields of goldenrod in

the stifling heat of September
Somehow
it seems to destroy us

It is only in isolate flecks that
something
is given off

No one
to witness
and adjust, no one to drive the car

The ostensible message here is that America is so lacking in rootedness (all those eccentric, inbred localities with 'no / peasant traditions') so lacking any cultural centre ('no one to drive the car') that its 'products' accept a cheap mass-produced culture which only serves to underline more starkly the hunger for some authentic meaning ('while the imagination strains'). In this light Elsie is a pitiable victim. But one might ask why it should be the young slatterns and Elsie who are made to bear so much of the weight of presenting this picture. The poem dwells with prurient pity on 'promiscuity', on the 'succumbing' under the hedge, most of all on the abject, unintellingent, passive fluidity of Elsie. The effect of this fallen femininity is damaging: it is 'as if the earth under our feet / were / an excrement of some sky': the earth, locus of the feminine: Williams, it will be recalled, had referred to the 'lack of attachment between the male and an objective world – to *the earth under feet*' (my emphasis) in his *Egoist* letter. The female's disconnection from the earth is an index of the depth of America's *malaise*. Yet the poem does not see women as the last bastion of rootedness. On the contrary, their passivity seems to render them the easiest and most vulnerable victims. On the basis of what we have seen so far, it would be reasonable to assume that what Elsie, and America, require, is the intervention of the imaginative male who can combine a sensitivity to the particular ('isolate flecks') with a properly constituted generalizing faculty ('to drive the car').

This impression is confirmed in *Paterson*, where in Book I we are given the story of the Rev. Hopper Cumming and his wife Mrs Sarah Cumming in 1812. They had walked up to the Passaic Falls to admire the view and, as they were on the point of leaving, Mrs Cummings had fallen to her death. Williams comments: 'A false language. A true. A false language pouring – a / language (misunderstood) pouring (misinterpreted) without / dignity, without minister, crashing upon a stone ear.'[43] The true language is the pouring of the waters, taken as a metaphor for language that arises from contact with particulars ('Earth, the chatterer, father of all / speech'.[44] The false language is that of the minister's wife who has not been true to her natural, feminine kinship with the waters of particularity: it is false because it is a perversion of the truth ('a / language (misunderstood)') under the influence of the minister's bad masculine generalities. Yet it should have been his instructive task to provide her with a true language by means of the desirable imaginative synthesis of particular and general. As it is, she is 'without minister'. The true relation between male and female is one of domination and subordination, a relation usefully allegorized at the beginning of *Paterson*, Book II:

> The scene's the Park
> upon the rock,
> female to the city
> – upon whose body Paterson instructs his thoughts
> (concretely)[45]

V

Like Pound, then, Williams espouses a poetics of control, closely linked to certain traditional notions of gender, and partly concealed by declarations of humility towards the object. But unlike Pound, Williams takes this humility so far as to link it with an overt reverence for the concreteness of the female – a reverence which, as I have tried to show, is quite ambivalent. It is not surprising, in the light of these facts, to find that the alleged 'openness' of Williams's forms must be carefully qualified. Take the convenient example of 'For Elsie'.

One must note the firm, discursive control of the theme. The poem as a whole is an almost urbane, discursive essay, beginning with a large general statement of considerable address: a good, firm opening, which the rest of the poem proceeds to illustrate and qualify. Diction is straightforward: a narrowly focused register, which cannot encourage complexity of verbal effects. The authoritative discursive air, on the contrary, encourages us to accept as irrefutable the demeaning tone of the patronizing sympathy for Elsie. The poem ends with the same neatness and address with which it had begun, where the authoritative generalizations, fine though they be, complete the effect of closure, snapping shut with a most memorable epigram. Whether it be in point of diction, of argumentative style, or of the treatment of the beginning or, more especially, the end, the poem is best described as 'closed'. Indeed, only our suspicion of the metaphor of 'open form' will prevent us from speaking of 'closed form'. (The absence of punctuation, if it has any effect at all, is delusive.) This poem is by no means atypical. Of course, there is no reason, apart from a certain kind of Modernist prejudice, to reject the discursive, and Williams, as here, often manages a finely turned, memorable assertiveness. Nor is there any reason in principle, by the way, speaking of Modernist prejudice, to reject his frequent recourse to the language of 'the heart'. But in any case it is true to say that, contrary to the received impression, Williams is more interesting as a prosodist (when properly understood) than for any 'openness', whether of treatment or form.

5

THE AMERICAN THING

I

'I like to describe things,' says Marianne Moore. The thing becomes an obsession in much American poetry during the first sixty years of the twentieth century, especially among those who feel an affinity with Pound, or come under his influence. Marianne Moore belongs to the former very select group, since, like Williams, she worked out her own way on a path running in some ways quite close to Pound's. But she is pungently individual. She must be the most obvious Anglo-American exponent, before the British Metaphor Men, of a kind of *Dingheit* that seeks, in striking metaphor or simile, an analogue for the way things look. Yet no more than they does she give the impression of cool neutrality, even though there is a kind of coolness unknown to them in her undemonstrative tone, thoughtful discursiveness, stately urbanity, and well-mannered scrupulous syntax. In fact, her similes and metaphors, though they clutch very successfully, in passing, at the visual similitudes they would convey, are frequently exotic or incongruous in their provenance or associations: the poem weaves a fantastic dance around its subject, even while that dance traces a visual impression of striking verisimilitude. These lines from 'The Jerboa' describe the creature in characteristic fashion:

> plunder its food store,
>   and you will be cursed. It

honors the sand by assuming its color;
   closed upper paws seeming one with the fur
   in its flight from a danger.

By fifths and sevenths,
in leaps of two lengths,
   like the uneven notes
   of the Bedouin flute, it stops its gleaning
      on little wheel castors, and makes fern-seed
      footprints with kangaroo speed.

Its leaps should be set
to the flageolet;
   pillar body erect
   on a three-cornered smooth-working Chippendale
      claw – propped on hind legs, and tail as third toe,
      between leaps to its burrow.[1]

Bedouin flutes, wheel castors, flageolets, Chippendale: the variety and incongruity of such vehicles of similitude, though they render their quota of visual precision, amount to a strange, substantial and not notably jerboal array. Yet one does not feel Moore's quiet exuberance in this kind as an intrusion on her subject: she keeps a respectful distance from the world she describes. Another poem conveys the same qualities:

THE FISH

wade
through black jade.
   Of the crow-blue mussel shells, one keeps
   adjusting the ash heaps;
      opening and shutting itself like

an
injured fan.
   The barnacles which encrust the side
   of the wave, cannot hide
      there for the submerged shafts of the

sun,
split like spun

> glass, move themselves with spotlight swiftness
> into the crevices —

Black jade, crow-blue, ash-heaps, an injured fan, spun glass. Again, variety and incongruity, but again the respectful distance. How is this achieved? In this poem the title becomes part of the first sentence. This makes the fish seem like a thing to be defined, of which the poem is the definition. This small air of objectivity would not add up to much were it not for other, more telling, factors peculiar to Moore's verse. The syllabic measure, for instance, itself imparts a sense of having no designs upon the subject. Its order does not conform to the natural rhythm of the speech, nor indeed does it even exist in the same dimension. For this reason it is also unable to participate in any onomatopoeic fitting of rhythm to sense. So even when Moore achieves a mimetic rhythm, as in the leaping cadences of 'The Jerboa', this has nothing to do with her metre, which is excluded from contributing to a sense of organic form. Indeed, both in its relationship to speech rhythm and in the way it is laid out it suggests 'mechanical form'. It seems fitting that the type-writer should have contributed to the placing of all those striking and sometimes intricate indentations. The rhymes, too, seem arbitrary, the mere observance of pattern; constant *enjambement* deprives them of sali-ence, and many, like the 'an' in stanza two, are unstressed. A good illustration of Moore's attitude to rhyme is to be found later in the poem:

> all the physical features of
> ac-
> cident — lack
> of cornice, dynamite grooves, burns, and
> hatchet strokes, these things stand
>   out on it.

Here the syllable 'ac-' fulfils its function punctiliously, but its position in the middle of a word shows that this is all it is asked to do.

In sum, Moore thinks of form as a delightful machine to be imposed on the subject-matter, with which it does not interfere. But even detachment may be eloquent: her attitude implies that the world is a body of facts or events which cannot be altered by the poem's activity. The many general statements in her poems (she is by no means a poet who can only look) tend to support this view. They often assert a state of affairs or a truth which is universally acknowledged: 'To wear the arctic fox / you have to kill it' ('The Arctic Ox (or Goat)'); 'Black in blazonry means / prudence' ('The Buffalo'); 'this cone / of the Pompeys which is known / / now as the Popes'' ('The Jerboa') Moore's poems do not convey interpretation of the world. They treat it as a given. So much of a given, in fact, that its appearance and nature can be seen as a matter of social consensus. What her poems do is to offer an eccentric imagination – eccentric in the strict sense: recognizing a social consensus, they adopt a quirky view in relation to it. It is as if she should say, 'You see this thing: we can agree on how it looks, even though my associations with how it looks are a little unusual. They are, nevertheless, drawn from a mind possessing a curious encyclopaedic knowledge of the facts that compose the world.' There is a modesty about this attitude. But it leaves the world and the self essentially disjunct. And the self is very much the ratiocinative ego. In keeping with this, one feels that Coleridge would have used the word Fancy rather than Imagination of her poems. The impulse to modernity and her Christianity (in that God has ordained things as they are) have co-operated to provide the conditions of existence of this poetry.

II

The heir and developer of Pound and Williams is Charles Olson. Like Williams he seeks to depict immediate experience, but his approach is far more radical. A more exact way of putting it might be to say that Olson wishes to convey the process of the energy of experience prior to reflective conceptualization. His is a 'radical empiricism', reminiscent of William James. As with James one can perceive analogies with Husserl, especially in the 'bracketing' of pure experience. These conceptions belong to a recognizably post-Romantic discourse, with strong specific American features, as a glance at Olson's theories reveals.

First, his concept of 'Composition by Field', as elaborated in the essay

'Projective Verse'. It is opposed to 'inherited line stanza, overall form' – a phrase in which traditional form is associated with inheritance – leaving open the question whether there are other things, including 'openness', that may be inherited.[2] In any case, this idea is felt to leave the poem free to express the 'energy' of the poet: 'A poem is energy transferred from where the poet got it . . . by way of the poem itself to, all the way over to, the reader. Okay. Then the poem must, at all points, be a high energy-construct and, at all points, an energy-discharge.'[3]

Again the Modernist ruse: the attempt to give an air of novel technical prestige to a fundamentally organicist and vitalist conception by recourse to an analogy with modern physics. Of course, such analogies, whether or not one takes them seriously, might bear fruit in productive new modes of writing. This does seem to be true of some aspects of Olson's work.

But Olson's scientism collapses in the next paragraph:

> This is the problem which any poet who departs from closed form is specifically confronted by. And it involves a whole series of new recognitions. From the moment he ventures into FIELD COMPOSITION – put himself into the open – he can go by no track other than the one the poem under hand declares, for itself.[4]

To put oneself in the open, to go by a track: here the field has ceased to refer to physics and become a pasture, or even a prairie frontier. Passing swiftly over the assertion that 'FORM IS NEVER MORE THAN AN EXTENSION OF CONTENT' (the Romantic provenance of this notion scarcely needs a mention) and glancing swiftly at the idea of breath as the source of syllable and line,[5] it is worth halting at that passage in the essay where Olson praises the machine that can most accurately and scientifically, while at the same time spontaneously, transcribe the poet's energy: the typewriter:

> from the machine has come one gain not yet sufficiently observed or used, but which leads directly on toward projective verse and its consequences. It is the advantage of the typewriter that, due to its rigidity and its space precisions, it can, for a poet, indicate exactly the breath, the pauses, the

suspensions even of syllables, the juxtapositions even of parts of phrases, which he intends. For the first time the poet has the stave and the bar a musician has had. For the first time he can, without the convention of time and meter, record the listening he has done to his own speech and by that one act indicate how he would want any reader, silently or otherwise to voice his work.[6]

The typewriter is that machine which can inscribe the precise, determinate hieroglyphic, in the form of the accurately spaced poem, for the pure process of experience. All this may seem a long way from the steam-trains whistling through wild American glades in the texts discussed by Leo Marx in *The Machine in the Garden*. But this 'field' which disguises itself as a concept of physics, and is accurately delineated only by a machine, belongs in the same category of a specifically American ambivalence about the encounter between the organic and the mechanical: one where the machine is given its due as an agent of progress, but must be kept subordinate to human life conceived in radically vitalist terms.

Olson's hieroglyph, or living letter, is best seen in the light of his admiration for the 'glyphs' of the Maya: 'a Sumer poem or Maya glyph is more pertinent to our purposes than anything else, because each of these people & their workers had forms which unfolded directly from content.'[7] The glyph is Olson's version of the ideogram, and like its forerunner it conveys direct reference, while retaining a certain distance from the object: 'the glyphs never got out of hand . . . as did the architecture and the pots, running, to naturalism . . . the way they kept the abstract alert.'[8] This distance represents a refusal to surrender the processes of one's own being to static contemplation of, or torpid intimacy with, objects. And such an attitude may seem appropriate. For the first glyphs adorned the phallus. The theory is propounded in a letter to Cid Corman (10 June 1951) from Lerma, Mexico, where Olson was studying the Maya. He begins by explaining that the 'herms', or heads of Hermes, found at crossroads in Greece, were originally phalluses. He then reveals his hunch that the Mayan *stelae*, on which he thought the glyphs he was studying were first inscribed, were '*herms !*'[9]

The vitally phallic poem is an 'open form'. It is supposed to represent the process of experience without hindrance, closure or treasonous formulation. Despite the fact that 'open form' is a metaphor which, even when allowed its quota of literal reference, can only point to a relative condition, it must be said that Olson goes some way towards living up to its implications in the construction of his poems. Apart from the 'organic form' already described, 'openness' might refer to several actual features of poems: curt juxtaposition in the creation of meaning; an element of novel verisimilitude in representing the associative flow of thought; a certain unfinished sense in endings; and permitting or creating a play of meanings and associations. Olson quite frequently achieves the first three, less often the last.

His most obvious success is to be found in the volume of shorter poems, *In Cold Hell in Thicket*, in which 'The Kingfishers' is the most considerable achievement.[10] This poem interweaves descriptions of the nesting habits of the kingfisher; the 'E on the stone' from the omphalos at the temple of Delphi; French translations of parts of Mao Tse-tung's address to the Chinese Communist party in 1948; and a consideration of an Aztec burial ground. The purpose for which these data are brought together may be gauged from the following lines from Section I (part 2):

> I thought of the E on the stone, and of what Mao said
> la lumiere"
>   but the kingfisher
> de l'aurore"
>   but the kingfisher flew west
> est devant nous!
>   he got the color of his breast
> from the heat of the setting sun!
>
> The features are, the feebleness of the feet
>   (syndactylism of the 3rd & 4th digit)
> the bill serrated, sometimes a pronounced beak, the wings
> where the color is, short and round, the tail
> inconspicuous.

The reference to the 'E' on the omphalos refers to the (phallic) sources of the energy of Hellenic and thus of Western civilization, which in this respect are identical with the source of Amerindian civilization (compare the glyphs on the herms). Mao sees the light of the dawn ahead, but the kingfisher, by contrast, gets the colour of his breast from the setting sun: the renewal of civilization has its roots in the recovery of the light of origins, which it should not ignore, as Mao may be in danger of doing, and as the West does in ignoring the light of Amerindian culture. To these implications is added the apparent redundance of describing the kingfisher. From one point of view this performs the familiar, and here necessary, post-Romantic function of indicating the credible reality of a mind at work. From another point of view it performs the equally familiar post-Romantic function of concealing the figurative in the naturalistic: for this is not really just a description of kingfishers. The feebleness of the kingfisher's feet reminds one of the vulnerability of Aztec civilization to the depredations of the conquistadors, which are described in part 3 of Section I; and thus of the vulnerability of all cultures. But there is the further redundance of repeating the phrase 'but the kingfisher', which is one of several features leading away from direct statement and towards an aesthetic and rhetorical presentation of a mind delighting in its intensity. Others are the notable alliteration in 'The features are the feebleness of the feet', the neat interweaving of Mao's speech with Indian legends about the kingfisher's breast, and the rhythmic compactness and address of the whole.

The richness and force of this passage are characteristic of the accomplishment of this volume. They are not sufficiently appreciated in Britain, where judgements of Olson tend to be formed on the more readily available *Maximus Poems*, in which these qualities are not so evident. They are achieved by an extension of Pound's techniques. It has been claimed that Olson's objectivism leads to his 'Decentering the Image'. This is Joseph Riddel's contention in J. Harari's *Textual Strategies*: Olson, as is there noted, claim to be replacing the 'classical representational' by the 'primitive abstract'.[11] The 'classical representational' is what is already formulated; the 'primitive abstract', an analogue of the Mayan glyph, is the representation of energy struggling into formulation but not attaining that finality. Or, to put it another way, the mind does not stop in its tracks long enough to bring an image to completion. This concept, then, is far from living up to the anti-logocentrism claimed for it: it derives from a nostalgia for a point of origin prior to language. But there is scant need to trouble with the question. The idea of a decentered image rests on the mystical belief that there is such an entity as an image outside the textual strategies which lead us to adopt that vague but useful word. Olson's images may seem decentered because he is able, often convincingly, to suggest the mind moving from point to point at some speed, raising an idea only to move on to the next, splicing and interweaving one idea with another, in a manner which owes much to Pound. To speak of decentred images is pretentious or unreflective sophistry.

And there is another side to Olson. For much of his poetry, especially in *The Maximus Poems*, is marked by an assertiveness which is direct, and relatively uncomplicated, even allowing for the elements of juxtapositional technique. This assertiveness goes hand in hand with a blunt, straightforward diction. The effect is to limit any sense of play and openness, and sometimes to achieve an oppressive, narrow effect, as in the swaggering statements of received notions of gender identity:

> The waist of a lion
> for a man to move properly
>
> And for a woman,
> who should move lazily,
> the weight of breasts
>
> This is the exercise for the morning[12]

Many of these statements qualify the condition of being 'a man': ' "You rectify what can be rectified," and when a man's heart / cannot see this, the door of his divine intelligence is shut.'[13] This overbearing stance is supported by the idea of Maximus, the persona, to whom such utterances are attributed in the series that bears his name; large, inclusive and a writer of letters that are full of what might best be called opinions.

It seems a trifle paradoxical, in view of the slightly modified egotism which pervades his works, that Olson should offer 'Objectism' as a general description of the stance implied by 'Projective Verse':

Objectism is the getting rid of the lyrical interference of the individual as ego, of the 'subject' and his soul, that peculiar presumption by which western man has interposed himself between what he is as as a creature of nature (with certain instructions to carry out) and those other creations of nature which we may, with no derogation, call objects.[14]

Read carefully, this offers two conceptions of humanity, as well as mentioning the world of objects: there is the 'creature of nature', and the lyrical ego which interferes with that creature's relationship with objects. We are back in familiar territory. It is scarcely surprising to find passages like this in *Maximus*, which seem to impugn not only social corruption, but even to suggest a mistrust of language itself:

> colored pictures
> of all things to eat: dirty
> postcards
> And words, words, words
> all, over everything
> No eyes or ears left
> to do their own doings (all
>
> invaded, appropriated, outraged, all senses
>
> including the mind, that worker on what is[15]

Equally, the social appears as a threat to the individual's hopes of acquiring an authentic way, in life or in poetry, which is to say an authentic encounter with the world of objects:

> We pick
>
> a private way
> among debris
> of common
> wealths – Public
> fact as sure
> as dimensions stay
> personal. And one desire,
> that the soul
> be naked
> at the end
>
> of time[16]

A natural corollary of this belief is the attribution of pure perception to 'the few': 'Polis now / is a few'.[17] Equally society's historical dimension, tradition, is to be mistrusted. Going into 'the open' is an escape from influence: a temporal movement towards nakedness.

All of this rests on an American Adamic conception, and it is right to say so. Yet it would be naive and wrong to see Olson as recommending an escape from history into some idealized Earthly Paradise. The extent to which *The Maximus Poems* offer the history and geography of Gloucester as Maximus's temporal and spatial context is sufficient to indicate that the neo-Adamic state Olson has in mind is an authentic, non-traditional relationship of the individual to the time and place that impinges on him. The character of this relationship can be gauged from *A Bibliography on America for Ed Dorn*, in which Olson describes, with the help of a diagram, the field of time and space which surrounds Dorn – 'MILLENNIA', 'PROCESS', 'QUANTITY' and 'PERSON'. This last, also described as 'THE INDIVIDUAL', is conceived as a particular, unique field on which the events and objects in the larger field act in a unique fashion, dictated by the particular position the individual occupies within it. A consequence of this is an emphasis on the undesirability of trying to leap over the field, so to speak, into premature generalization: the true way to knowledge is to start from one's particular place in the field: all other things will be added unto this. And so he begins to sum up by advising Dorn: 'Best thing to do is *to dig one thing or place or man* until you yourself know more abt that than is possible to any other man. It doesn't matter whether it's Barbed Wire or Pemmican or Paterson or Iowa. But *exhaust* it. Saturate it. Beat it. And then u KNOW everything else very fast: one saturation job (it might take 14 years).'[18] If this recalls Keats's insistence on particular experience – even if it goes beyond it in its indebtedness to Whitehead's mediations of concepts of modern physics – that is probably no accident. In particular, Olson admired Keats's doctrine of Negative Capability, with its rejection of 'reaching after fact and reason'.[19] But if, for Keats, the true poet is a chameleon, for Olson poet and person realize their authentic nature as objects among others. The person might be defined as that object which is open to the space–time process in general. Such openness permits the transmission of energies without blocking or falsification. Or: 'man as object in field of force declaring self as force because is force in exactly such relation & can accomplish expression of self as force.'[20] This is our proper paradise: to enter the energies of matter in our true being, as one of those energies: 'matter is . . . the world which prevents, but once felt, enables your being to have its heaven.'[21] Here, then, is another secularized version of the Romantic achievement of transcendence through a probing and piercing of the resistant surface of Nature.

III

Olson, then, is a dogmatizer who praises openness. There is an ambiguity about his attitude to authority which can be paralleled in his attitude to the two most prominent characters in Melville's *Moby Dick*, Ahab and Ishmael. In his perceptive study of this, *Call me Ishmael*, Olson reveals his affiliation to the voluminously open mind of Ishmael:

> Like the Catskill eagle Ishmael is able to dive down into the blackest gorges and soar out to the light again.
> . . .
> [He] has that cleansing ubiquity of the chorus in all drama . . . It was Ishmael who learned the secrets of Ahab's blasphemies from the prophet of the fog, Elijah. He recognized Pip's God-sight, and moaned for him. He cries forth the glory of the crew's humanity. Ishmael tells *their* story and *their* tragedy as well as Ahab's and thus creates the *Moby-Dick* in which the Ahab world is . . . *included*.[22]

Ahab, by contrast, is a closed mind, narrowly, vengefully and obsessively focused on the drive for domination: 'In the Ahab-world there is no place for "converse with the Intelligence, Power, the Angel".'[23] Now Melville links both Ahab and Ishmael to phallic imagery. Ishmael is seen in terms of the phallic as sign for the endlessness and freedom of desire. As he says: 'For small erections may be finished by their first architects; grand ones, true ones, ever leave the copestone to posterity. God keep me from ever completing anything. This whole book is but a draught – nay, but the draught of a draught.'[24] But Ahab, 'dismasted', with a stump of whale-bone replacing one of his legs, represents a perverted narrowness and definition of desire. Yet Olson himself is well able to describe and explain the tragic sublimity Melville imparts to Ahab. He sees it in terms of Shakespeare's tragic heroes, especially Macbeth. And the obvious echoes of Faust and Milton's Satan link the depiction of Ahab's dominating spirit to a suspecting view of the project of post-Renaissance civilization, not least as found in America: Moby Dick is compared to 'the White Steed of the Prairies'.[25] Despite Olson's desire to set himself apart from the dominating spirit, he may have gazed at it too long, like Ahab contemplating the whale.

These two aspects, the relatively closed and the relatively open, are reflected in the way Olson divides his page when writing poetry. Paul Christensen has shown how the 'horizontal axis, running from left margin to right, marks the range of the poet's thought from objective utterance to haziest reverie':[26] an extraordinary resuscitation of the dialectic in Coleridge's Conversation Poems. But there is no need to be aware of that remote relation to see how the novel aspects of this use of the page provide new expressive materials for poetry. Olson's graphic poetics in general have encouraged, and probably will continue to encourage, all kinds of confident movements around the page. Nevertheless, the effects procured can be equivocal or uninteresting unless reinforced by a reasonably systematic symbolism of space, such as Olson had in mind. Does the totality of the technical means he employs succeed in representing the process of experience? It depends on what 'representing' means. There are all kinds of plausible ways of signifying a naturalism about this process (or, if you like, about the stream of consciousness) within the space created by markers representing verisimilitude and absence of markers foregrounding artifice. But there is no apodictic signifier for the truth of mental process: representation remains representation. This fact had already been made part of the subject of *Ulysses* by Joyce, but for reasons of its attachment to a transparent signifier the Pound tradition is impervious to the lesson.

So it is probably otiose to carp at some of the passages in *Maximus* that sound much more like fully formulated dogmatizing than the mind moving through pure moments on the first border of signification. Thus, in discussing Bowditch in Letter 16:

> It is said for example, that it is he himself
>   (about to start on his fourth voyage,

he wrote to his future wife,
    fr Boston, 22 July 1799
'It was with the greatest difficulty
we obtained our complement of men,
& a curious set of them it is:
Tinkers, Tailors, Barbers, Country
schoolmasters, one old Greenwhich
Pensioner, a few negroes, mulattoes
Spaniards &c &c &c but they will do
well enough when properly disciplined'

who was the first 'trustee' of others' monies
who treated them as separate from his own accounts.
In other words, he marks that most neglected of all
economic law: how the coming into existence of benevolence
(the 19th century, left and right)
is the worst, leads to the worst, breeds
what we have[22]

Leaving aside the quotation, obviously there is no rule which precludes Olson's contribution to this being poetry – at least, no rule which would preclude it on the grounds of its mere discursiveness. Indeed, one of the good effects of reading Olson might be to discourage certain types of Modernist prejudice in favour of compulsory intensity and lyricism. Of course, one might have doubts as to the aesthetic interest of this passage. But that is a different matter. However, as far as Olson's intention to demonstrate the process is concerned, there is no way in which such a demonstration can be either verified or falsified. The fact that this is a discursive passage of no especial eccentricity, whether benign or malign, only makes this more obvious. One may take Olson's word for it that it represents the pure process of his mind at work. But his word finds no special objective corroboration within the passage, and thus cannot alter either our perception of the passage or our sense of what it means to depict the mental process. It is clear, of course, that the parts justified to the left-hand margin are continuous with each other, so that the passage in the middle of the page represents a flash of memory: a remembered fact about Bowditch. So we have a novel signifier for a moment of memory: indentation. This accords with the plan for the page described by Christensen. But even so, beyond this there is little to differentiate the middle passage from the rest.

Of course, Olson might claim that the processes of his mind are both uniquely special and, at the same time, representative of humanity in general. Some such Romantic claim is surely implied. But there is no reason in principle to take the idea of the truthful depiction of the mind seriously. It denies the necessity of the signifier. The only good thing that might emerge from such an ambition would be novel and illuminating ways of signifying the mind at work. As to the interest of the signifiers Olson does muster, we have seen that typography, open-endedness and radical juxtaposition are all areas where he shows originality. His graphic poetics, in particular, provide an opening for future poetry of a kind which he perhaps could not foresee. For however much one may seek to attribute some settled auditory meaning to his positioning of lines on the page, that positioning remains hard to assimilate to the mysticism of voice and breath which is its intended basis. These poetics are, then, irreducibly graphic, in the sense that the element governed by the eye alone is highly significant and cannot be removed without the poem becoming a different thing. On the other hand the frequently discursive mode of his poetry, though not an offence against any canon, is neither original nor complex, and the assertive dogmatism of much of *Maximus* is oppressive and narrow.

IV

The fact that an attempt to depict the pure process of experience takes no necessary form, and is certainly not bound to anything like an Olsonian one, can be gauged from the work of the 'Objectivists', Louis Zukofsky and George Oppen. Both were in touch with each other and with Williams and Carl Rakosi in the late twenties, and the group takes its name from the 1932 *An "Objectivists" Anthology*, edited by Zukofsky, whose theories reveal many presuppositions and prejudices that recall Olson's. Thus, of the connection between science and poetry:

To think clearly about poetry it is necessary to point out that its aims and those of science are not opposed; and that only the more complicated, if not finer, tolerances of number, measure and weight that define poetry make it seem imprecise as compared to science, to quick readers of instruments. It should be said rather that the most complicated standards of science – including definitions, laws of nature and thematic constructions – are poetic.[28]

And words directly represent experience: 'The economy of presentation in writing is a reassertion of faith that the combined letters – the words – are absolute symbols for objects, states, acts, interrelations, thoughts about them.'[29] And there is the recognition that typography might be a means of assisting an ideogrammatic method at the levels both of sound and sight: 'Typography – certainly – if print and arrangement of it will help tell how the voice should sound. It is questionable on the other hand whether the letters of the alphabet can be felt as the Chinese feel their written characters.'[30]

Zukofsky's adherence to the idea of the real, or objective, is, if anything, more puritanical than that of any of the post-Poundians. He had translated René Taupin's 'Three Poems by André Salmon' in *Poetry* in an issue he edited in 1931, and these lines are revealing about his own attitudes: 'The first requisite was to avoid the betrayal of words and emotions, so that the real would strike the poet directly . . . The most direct contact is obligatory, more striking than any metaphor tainted with impure interpretation.'[31]

Zukofsky himself is suspicious of the modern quest for myth, for metaphor writ large, where Pound and Olson are not:

The poet wonders why so many today have raised up the word 'myth', finding the lack of so-called 'myths' in our time a crisis the poet must overcome or die from . . . when instead a case can be made for the poet giving some of his life to the use of the words *the* and *a*: both of which are weighted with as much epos and historical destiny as one man can perhaps resolve. Those who do not believe this are too sure that the little words mean nothing among so many other words.[32]

This passage reveals a hostility towards the generalizing treachery of myth, its flight from the uncategorizable real. It commends the examination of language's representations at their least pretentious and least falsifying: at the level of 'economy of presentation'. Zukofsky is equally radical in his approach to that other, unsettling, aspect of language, the expressive, desiring the greatest possible fidelity to the poet's breath and music, a fact to which his translations of Catullus are the most striking testimony.[33] For in these he seeks to reproduce not merely the meaning, but the very rhythms and even phonetic pattern – in literal terms of consonants and vowels – of the original.

Yet this purist approach to the fine edge of encounter between words and experience raises many problems, precisely because of its seriousness. The interest in the words 'a' and 'the', for example, is not merely indicative of a care for 'little words', but also of an awareness of the importance of articles, as well as nouns, at least in English. But this awareness undermines the nominalist implications of some of Zukofsky's other remarks, revealing some grasp of the fact that language cannot provide a direct reflection of the real. This grasp is evident in other, more general, remarks: 'How much what is sounded by words has to do with what is seen by them – and how much what is at once sounded and seen by them crosscuts an interplay among themselves – will naturally sustain the scientific definition of poetry we are looking for.'[34] This is not clear. First the relationship between 'sounding' and 'seeing' is raised, then immediately dropped; whereupon the two activities are assumed to go together as one element in language, which 'crosscuts' another 'interplay', that between word and word according to other qualities than 'sounding' and 'seeing'. Nevertheless, two things are perhaps clear: 'sounding' in words is an important element in the meaning of poetry; and so is interplay, which gives a picture of meaning as created, in some undefined way, by aspects of language irreducible to the idea of reflection, probably by a Mallarmean interaction of connotations.

This far from reductionist approach to meaning is exemplified in Zukofsky's long poem *A*, where music and the musical qualities of language are frequent themes.[35] It is ostensibly about one of those little words, the indefinite article: an immense poem about classifying something as one of a kind, and by virtue of this alone, one that makes much of the fact that denoting something is not a simple matter of reflection or indication. But the poem also devotes much time to the associations evoked by the letter A itself: by its shape, its sound, places where it is prominently displayed, and so on. In doing so it exploits precisely those areas of 'sounding' and 'interplay' that complicate the Imagist model for Zukofsky. Even so, one would not expect him to relinquish his objectivism. Because the indefinite article is normally followed by a noun, the title gives the impression that the whole poem is an enormously inflated noun, or at least a definition. The fact that the poem is also 'z-sited', as he announces in the last line, implies both the end of utterance and the end of his own particular utterance: Z for Zukofsky.[36] So the poem is a truthful naming by an individual.

Nevertheless, the idea of music is behind its structure: Zukofsky thinks of it as a kind of fugue: one section responds to another in the fugal sense of treating the same subject in a different key (metaphorically speaking); there are countersubjects, that is to say contrasting thematic elements that recur. In practice a strict pattern is seldom used in the employment of this basic idea, and Zukofsky conforms to his model in this respect also. But the use of fugal structure in the architecture of a literary work does not carry such strong, specifically musical associations as the traditional ones of rhythm, assonance and so on. The analogue may have helped Zukofsky to write, of course. But another way of looking at it is simply to say that he uses the ideogrammatic method. Pound himself thought of the large-scale use of this method in the *Cantos* as fugal. As Yeats confides to us in 'A Packet for Ezra Pound' in the second version of *A Vision*:

> he explains that it will, when the hundredth canto is finished, display a stcture like that of a Bach Fugue ... He has scribbled on the back of an envelope certain sets of letters that represent emotions or archetypal events − I cannot find any adequate definition − A B C D and then J K L M, and then each set of letters repeated, and then A B C D inverted and this repeated, and then a new element X Y Z ...[37]

This is an adequate definition of Zukofsky's procedure. It may readily be grasped in the structure of 'A-1'. First we are presented with the performance of Bach's *St Matthew Passion* in Leipzig with the composer himself as choirmaster. Then we are given the response, a treatment of the same subject in a different key: this is the presentation of the performance of the same work in twentieth-century New York, in

Carnegie Hall. The countersubject appears when the speaker, leaving the
Hall, encounters a ragged tramp and hears the pretentious chatter of
some of the concert-goers: the countersubject, then, is the relationship
between culture and the modern economic order, treated in such a way
that a sense of disconnection between them emerges, and a sense of
moral and cultural emptiness. The indictment becomes explicit when we
encounter the figure of Mr Magnus, the industrialist: 'We ran 'em in
chain gangs, down in the Argentine.'

Texture as much as architectonics recalls Pound:

> Far into (about three) in the morning,
> The trainmen wide awake, calling
> Station on station, under earth,
>
> *Cold stone above Thy head.*
> *Weary, broken bodies.*
> *Sleeping: their eyes were full of sleep.*
>
> The next day the reverses
> As if the music were only a taunt:
> As if it had not kept, flower-cell, liveforever,
>   before the eyes, perfecting.
> – I thought that was finished:
> Existence not even subsistence,
> Worm eating bark of the street tree,
> Smoke sooting skyscraper chimneys

The rhythm, particularly the strong rhythm of the compact descriptive
lines quoted last; the interjection of a lyrical quotation; and the lyrical
evocation of the beauty of the pattern in art – all are very Poundian in
flavour, especially in their collation. The very idea of a perfect form
('flower-cell, liveforever') emerging from the world's particulars is itself
Poundian. Paul Smith, in *Pound Revised*, severely qualifies the comparison: 'whereas in Pound the realisation of that "forma" is *given*, a
metaphysical event of epiphany, what *A* is working towards is a piece of
writing, a particular form of language.'[38] It may be helpful to para-
phrase this perceptive remark. In the *Cantos* our sense that the details
bind together is cajoled by Pound's insistence on the Eleusis – Confucius
connection, and by what it means about the right ordering of the
circuits of exchange in sexuality and economy. What at first seems like a

fortuitous detail is often coralled into this system in the end. Thus are we invited to accede to Pound's ideas: 'look at the chaotic details of the world; to me, the poet, they look exactly the same, witness the chaos in this poem; yet gradually my insight has made their sense emerge without any imposition.' Such is the disingenuous ploy to which the loyal Poundian must submit. But in Zukofsky's poem, consistently with his mistrust of myth, there is no sense of a veiled, anterior system. The pattern of art really is the pattern of the poet's aesthetic discoveries, and in this sense the poem is an object (an important meaning of 'Objectivism' for its adherents). It seems no accident that this humility is combined with an evocation of human love which, in any detail, is far more convincing than any single comparable line in the whole of Pound's work:

> Blest
> Ardent   good,
> Celia,   speak simply, rarely   scarce, seldom –
> Happy, immeasurable love[39]

How unfortunate, then, that intentions and dispositions may count for so little in literature! Zukofsky's engaging personality and considered intention to write an impersonal musical poetry of experience seem on the face of it a more fertile propagator of poetry than Pound's poisonous brew of aesthetic, political and sexual fascism. Yet the texture of the two poets' work is similar enough in most respects, and Pound is capable of much greater energy. And however suspect the sources of his attempts at coherence, the reader is unlikely to forfeit respect for their results. It is impossible to conceive of a writing that foreswears such attempts. To dub them metaphysical is to evoke a tangle of philosophical problems, but one may surely say, at least, that many of the connections we make in matters of highest value must be metaphysical.

V

George Oppen displays an interest in the minute texture of events both minute and not-so-minute. In this he begs comparison with Williams and Olson. But he, most of all, shows what different results the pursuit of the objective may have for different observers. Like Zukofsky he displays a serious-mindedness which abhors facileness. In his case this results in a poetry which renders the mundane mysterious, cryptic and sometimes bizarre. The sense of alienation informs modern writing so often that familiarity with it may breed indifference. Not so with Oppen, whose odd-angled and fragmented view is intensified by explicit references to the modern alienated condition, whether through the ubiquitous and obvious image of the separating window, or through overt statement:

> We are not coeval
> With a locality
> But we imagine others are,
>
> We encounter them. Actually
> A populace flows
> Thru the city.
>
> This is a language, therefore, of New York.[40]

There is a fascination with the machine, notwithstanding it is seen as part of the alienating environment, and contrasted with the organic, from which it is often emphatically set apart:

> The machine stares out,
> Stares out
> With all its eyes
>
> Thru the glass
> With the ripple in it, past the sill
> Which is dusty – If there is someone
> In the garden!
> Outside, and so beautiful.[41]

The machine and the garden are recurring symbols in Oppen's work. And women are associated with the garden or with vegetation. With these they share a relatively insentient mode of life which may stand them in good stead in the confusing and alienated modern world:

There are women

Radically alone in courage
And fear

Clear minded and blind

In the machines
And the abstractions and the power

Of their times as women can be blind

Untroubled by a leaf moving
In a garden

('A Kind of Garden')[42]

But Oppen is free of any general tendency to indulge in a discourse of power over objects and women. Rather, the feminine is identified with a part of himself which is struggling to make human sense of the modern world, 'the feminine technologies / Of desire / And compassion which will clothe / / Everyone' ('Technologies).[42] But neither good nor bad intentions can say everything about a poet. Oppen's success in conveying the mysterious nature of everyday experience may be gauged from his poems, especially those in his first collection, *Discrete Series* (1934), of which the following fragment – for that seems an appropriate word – is as representative an example as any:

The evening, water in a glass
Thru which our car runs on a higher road.

Over what has the air frozen?

Nothing can equal in polish and obscured
    origin that dark instrument
A car
    (Which.
Ease; the hand on the sword-hilt[44]

Like so many of Oppen's poems this refuses easy recuperation to an explanatory scenario. The 'discrete' moment is offered as an object, and the poem is the object that offers it without dishonesty. We appreciate the metaphor of water in a glass applied to the evening, and are inclined to picture the driver as appreciating that clarity from the 'higher road'. But the question, 'Over what has the air frozen?' indicates a sense of wonder at the strangeness of the scene below, as it might have been formulated on the spot, without deigning to provide us with naturalistic description. Suddenly, and almost inexplicably, the poem switches to reflection on the car. Like the evening, the car is polished and mysterious. Is this the point of the reflection? Is it the windows of the car that have made the evening like water in a glass? Perhaps. But this is a possibility one can play with rather than verify. And what about 'Which'? Is this a question, or is it a relative pronoun in the accusative, the verb 'Ease' being imperative? More likely the latter, permitting the rough translation: 'you should ease the car with your hand on the sword-hilt.' This makes the sword-hilt a credible metaphor for gear-stick. A possible deduction from the poem, then, is that it is a sophisticated description of the way modern technology both alienates, and at the same time imparts a sense of remote control which is especially congenial to traditionally masculine ways of thinking about power. Yet the poem will not relieve our uncertainty about this interpretation.

Like a Williams text this offers itself as naked speech. But there is no broad tonal wash of rhythm here. The rhythmic units are notably inconsistent with each other. We can naturalize the poem as curt, uncertain speech. But more useful for the purposes of appreciation is the way such curtness helps to enable a disjunction between the elements of the poem. It is Oppen rather than Williams or Pound who has most convincingly followed the analogy with Cubism. This becomes more obvious once one has grasped that he thinks of his data as experiences rather than material objects.

VI

One implication of this brief survey of some American poets of 'the Pound era' is, as might be expected, that there is no easily predictable relationship between adherence to certain traditional concepts of gender and the texture of the poetry itself. Even where, as in the case of Olson, a vauntingly phallic philosophy pervades everything, this may permit a

rich and playful poetry to the extent that it is understood as a philosophy about the endlessness of desire. That is also true of Pound. Yet the
phallocrats are dangerous teachers, not least to working poets. For where
their philosophy colludes with the ideology of the poet's privileged
perception or genius, the result can be as arid in literary terms as it is
theoretically doctrinaire. By the same token, ideas about the feminine as
organic, although they might not be accepted as a compliment by many
women, can serve to enrich the work of poets who regard the organic–
feminine as the locus of a complex, multi-dimensional response to
experience.

6

CHARLES TOMLINSON

I

In his 1966 introduction to Tomlinson's *The Necklace* (first published in 1955), Donald Davie remarks that 'the effect of reading these poems is quite unlike the effect of reading a volume by Stevens. It is even more unlike the effect of such other poets as Keats and Tennyson, who are both concerned in their different ways, as this poet is, to register sense-perceptions with exquisite precision'.[1] The difference is that Tomlinson's poems are 'anything but languorous or hectic or opulent'.[2] Where Keats's or Tennyson's poems, one might add, are concerned to describe the moods that are prompted or supported by particular sense-perceptions, Tomlinson permits his intense awareness of 'the mystery bodied over against [us] in the created universe' to dictate the mood and the thoughts.[3] His attitude implicitly aligns itself with Stevens's belief that the imagination must work on this world; that there is no 'haunt of prophecy' that has endured 'As April's green endures' ('Sunday Morning', IV).[4] The corollary for poetic practice is stated in 'To the One of Fictive Music', where we are told that 'That music is intensest which proclaims / The near, the clear', and 'That apprehends the most which sees and names . . . an image that is sure.' But he goes on to qualify this:

> Yet not too like, yet not so like to be
> Too near, too clear, saving a little to endow
> Our feigning with the strange unlike . . .

Stevens remains a Romantic, wishing to stress, whatever importance he accords to sensory experience, the essential ingredient of imagination. Indeed, the lines are strikingly reminiscent of Yeats's in 'To the Rose upon the Rood of Time'. But they are strangely reversed in effect. Yeats seeks solace in the rose of imagination:

> Come near, that no more blinded by man's fate,
> I find under the boughs of love and hate,
> In all poor foolish things that live a day,
> Eternal beauty wandering on her way.

He has to remind himself not to forget 'common things':

> Come near, come near, come near – Ah, leave me still
> A little space for the rose-breath to fill!
> Lest I no more hear common things that crave
> The weak worm hiding down in its small cave,
> The field-mouse running by me in the grass.

For Yeats, the visionary opens onto the transcendent ('Eternal beauty') and does not require validation. He feels secure enough with this to be able to stop and remind himself that he should also remain aware of 'common things'. For Stevens the world is clearly unencumbered with the transcendent, and the imagination must work on it unillusioned. But its activity is self-validating, and it maintains the vatic manner.

None of this gets us very far with Tomlinson, except to point a contrast. He lives in Stevens's heaven-bereft world. But he takes this to mean that there should be no divorce between imagination and clarity about the world. It is easy to see this contrast if one compares Tomlinson's 'Nine Variations in a Chinese Winter Setting', from *The Necklace*, with the Stevens poem to which it alludes, 'Thirteen Ways of Looking at a Blackbird'. Stevens makes the blackbird the occasion for exhibiting thirteen consciousnesses or points of view, and it is as important for him to register the tone of the consciousness as to note the impression of the blackbird. Thus,

> Icicles filled the long window
> With barbaric glass.
> The shadow of the blackbird
> Crossed it, to and fro.
> The mood
> Traced in the shadow
> An indecipherable cause.

This is avowedly a matter of mood, and of the imagination seeking for causes. But for Tomlinson sense-perceptions are not the occasions of mood. Rather, they define it:

> The outline of the water-dragon
> Is not embroidered with so intricate a thread
> As that with which the flute
> Defines the tangible borders of a mood.

This is the most 'Romantic' of the 'Nine Variations'. The others concentrate on sense-perception for its own sake:

> Pine-scent
> In snow-clearness
> Is not more exactly counterpointed
> Than the creak of trodden snow
> Against a flute.

The employment of synaesthesia, as here, is redolent of Symbolism. But although that is where Tomlinson has learnt it, he has treated it to a typically Modernist ruse. Just as Modernism tends to extract Romantic sense-perception in general from the metaphysical gestures that surround it, so Tomlinson deprives Symbolist synaesthesia of its echoes of transcendence: it becomes a matter of exact recording, and how better to record these perceptions of the world than by converting them into the terms of another sense's perceptions? The constant presence of the flute is a pointer towards the attitude that eschews the 'full orchestra' of poetry.

This it does because the orchestra suggests the weight of emotive language and metaphysical speculation overpowering the simplicity and exactness of response to the world. As Tomlinson says in another poem from *The Necklace*, 'Through Binoculars', where he describes the abnormality of what we see with them,

> This fictive extension into madness
> Has a kind of bracing effect:
> That normality is, after all, desirable
> One can no longer doubt having experienced its opposite.
>
> Binoculars are the last phase in a romanticism.

Yes, it is simply 'normality' that is desirable, and the rest of the poem sees this as clear sense-perception: 'romanticism' is held to be averse from this. But note that it is said of binoculars that they are the '*last* phase in a romanticism' (my emphasis). They do not represent the full-blown article, then, but rather an intense attention to things that is of the wrong kind, because still more concerned with intensity than with deference towards the world: 'Definition grows clear-cut, but bodiless.' If Craig Raine and the Metaphor Men had been invented when Tomlinson wrote this poem, he might have had them in mind.

Charles Tomlinson is an accomplished writer of free verse. In this he has learnt from the Americans, especially from Williams. Which is fitting. For when he espoused Stevens's belief that 'That music is intensest which proclaims / The near, the clear', he did so by deciding that the best way to achieve this objective was to follow Williams's practice and subdue Stevens's full orchestra of music. Tomlinson has learnt much from Williams's experiments, while remaining healthily sceptical of their theoretical trappings: he refers to 'Williams's ... self-defeating attempts to define the "variable foot", that "relative measure" which ends by being ... a contradiction in terms.'[5] What Tomlinson has learnt from Williams is to seek a rhythm that is appropriate (nothing revolutionary there) while at the same time using the eye and its response to lineation to manipulate emphases. The appearance of words on the page is as important for him as for his mentor. This fact is well reflected in those short-lined poems which look most obviously American on the page, especially in those which reveal

Tomlinson's gift for gentle, humane comedy. A good example can be found in 'A Word in Edgeways', from *The Way of a World*:[6]

> I will not
> say that every literate male in
> America is a soliloquist, a
> ventriloquist, a strategic
> egotist, an inveterate
> campaigner—explainer over and
> back again on the terrain of him-
> self — what I will
> say is they are not un-
> interesting: they are simply
> unreciprocal and yes it was a
> pleasure if not an unmitigated
> pleasure and I yes I did enjoy our
> conversation goodnightthankyou

The lineation here succeeds in both expressing and distancing the subject: for it both enacts the breathless momentum of the talk and, by the emphases it creates, indicates a mildly censorious irony on the part of the speaker ('yes it was a / pleasure').

In general Tomlinson's lineation is less startling than Williams's: it works to support a careful accuracy of description, where in Williams it tends to focus unexpected attention on details that might otherwise have been ignored. The beginning of 'Swimming Chenango Lake' is especially characteristic of Tomlinson's longer poems:

> Where the first leaves at the first
>   Tremor of the morning have dropped
> Anticipating him, launching their imprints
>   Outwards in eccentric, overlapping circles.
> There is a geometry of water, for this
>   Squares off the clouds' redundancies

The emphasis on line-beginnings serves to heighten key elements in the description ('Tremor . . .', 'Onwards . . .', 'Squares off . . .') whereas in Williams the combination of short lines and unexpected emphasis looks far more analytic and distanced:

that brilliant field
of rainwet orange
blanketed

by the red grass
and oilgreen bayberry

the last yarrow
on the gutter
white by the sandy
rainwater[7]

Williams is concerned with minutely heightened perception; Tomlinson's lineation, both expressive and analytic, enacts the delicate relationship between perceiver and perceived that is his chief subject.

II

Tomlinson is much admired by some of those neo-Modernists who espouse the objective and recommend the elimination of metaphor from writing. And it does seem that, for Tomlinson and these admirers, too obtrusive a use of metaphor or simile detracts from the clarity of definition. The poet and critic Andrew Crozier contrasts Heaney's 'figurative' poetry unfavourably with the objectivity of Tomlinson. He quotes 'Geneva Restored' from *Seeing is Believing*,[8] asking us to note the 'careful sustained description of the city's environs, with its suggestion that language might be compatible with what it refers to rather than necessarily appropriated to the special register of the poet's sensibility':

Limestone, faulted with marble; the lengthening swell
Under the terraces, the farms in miniature, until
With its sheer, last leap, the Salève becomes
The Salève, just naked, the cliff which nobody sees
Because it pretends to be nothing, and has shaken off
Its seashore litter of house-dots. Beneath that,
This — compact, as the other is sudden, and with an inaccessible
Family dignity: close roofs on a gravel height,
Building knot into rock; the bird's nest of a place

> Rich in protestant pieties, in heroic half-truths
> That was Ruskin's.

Crozier comments:

> Not only is the poem's point of intersection with the world realised in detail, and in terms of particular, local qualities, the place is also remembered to possess a history, to be charged with it indeed as associations, with Protestantism, with Ruskin, which feed into the present. Yet none of these, it can be argued, owes its presence to the poet's intervention; they occur because the poet finds them interesting and they sustain the poem accordingly.[9]

And he concludes, in the same place, that Tomlinson's poem is 'highly literal, informed by respect for the presence and character of things'. But it should be obvious that the objectivity Crozier claims to find in Tomlinson sounds little different from the fidelity others profess to discover in a poet such as Heaney, who is seen by Crozier as one of the figurative and anti-literal. Indeed, so intrusively 'figurative' a poet as Craig Raine can talk of his own poetry as arising out of 'seeing things very clearly'.[10] Compare the title of Tomlinson's collection, *Seeing is Believing*. Crozier possesses a salutary sensitivity to the relationship between observer and observed. But, like so many objectivists, he is alarmingly naive in his use of words such as 'literal' and 'refers'. He undoubtedly overstates his case about Tomlinson, who can be shown to be quite 'unliteral' in certain respects. It is worth examining the question of his 'literalness', for there is no doubt that Tomlinson's avowed aim is to achieve something like this.

The best-known poem from *Seeing is Believing*, 'A Meditation on John Constable', presents the subject-matter of that great Romantic artist, with good reason, as 'Facts'. And it rightly insists that Constable was particularly interested in 'accidents', unusual states of light and weather, representing these, however, as indices of emotion:

> Facts. And what are they?
> He admired accidents, because governed by laws,
>   Representing them (since the illusion was not his end)
> As governed by feeling.

From the very beginning of the poem Tomlinson delightfully makes his point that description and 'passion' are inseparable by rendering 'facts' about clouds in painterly words:

> Clouds
> Followed by others, temper the sun in passing
>   Over and off it. Massed darks
> Blotting it back, scattered and mellowed shafts
>   Break damply out of them . . .
>   It shrinks to a crescent
> Crushed out, a still lengthening ooze
>   As the mass thickens, though cannot exclude
> Its silvered-yellow.

The painterliness of this passage insists on the appropriation art makes of its objects. Of course, Tomlinson's appropriation is not an obtrusive one: his ideal is a tactful and strenuous encounter between observer and object:

> Art
> Is complete when it is human. It is human
> Once the looped pigments, the pin-heads of light
>   Securing space under their deft restrictions
> Convince, as the index of a possible passion,
>   As the adequate gauge, both of the passion
> And its object.

That side of Constable that leans to expressiveness (here indicated by Tomlinson) can be exemplified in his admiration for the work of Alexander Cozens. In his *New Method of Assisting the Invention in Drawing Original Compositions of Landscape* (1785), Cozens remarks: 'It cannot be doubted that too much time is spent in copying the works of others, which tends to weaken the powers of invention.' And then, more unexpectedly, 'and I do not scruple to affirm, that too much time may be employed in copying the landscapes of Nature herself.'[11] One of Cozens's methods of 'assisting the invention' was the system of 'blotting': non-representational brush-strokes on a piece of paper, on the basis of which the artist invented a landscape.[12] It is intriguing to note that Tomlinson himself sometimes employs a similar method in his own painting.[13] The 'objectivity' of both Constable and Tomlinson must be severely qualified. And Tomlinson is very aware of the kind of Constable on whom he is commenting. But the encounter in which he delights, of impassioned but objective observer with a landscape, does not move very far beyond that which subtends many descriptive passages in Wordsworth and Coleridge: the solitary interpreter, animating the landscape with a mixture of deference and energy. There is much, of course, in what Calvin Bedient says: 'In Tomlinson, the spirit, as if ignorant of what once sustained it – platonic forms, Jehovah, the Life Force, the whole pantheon of the metaphysical mind – finds bliss in trees and stones that are merely trees and stones.'[14] Yet even this characteristic does not put Tomlinson's spirit unequivocally at odds with Wordsworth's: recall that Riffaterre was capable of claiming that the message of Wordsworth's 'Yew-Trees' is 'Sensation is all'. The claim is false, but it is understandable. Conversely, in Tomlinson the pressure persists to find meaning, as well as bliss, in trees and stones. And since for him this meaning cannot be imposed by the observer, it sounds like an echo of transcendence: otherwise, where does it come from? Indeed, Tomlinson himself says of his early poetry, including *The Necklace* and *Seeing is Believing*, that, 'if . . . the tonality sounded American, the tradition of the work went back to Coleridge's conversation poems.'[15] Yet there is no 'almighty Spirit' in Tomlinson. What, then, constitutes the 'echo of transcendence'?

The poem 'The Atlantic', from *Seeing is Believing*, may help to provide an answer to this question:

> Launched into an opposing wind, hangs
>   Grappled beneath the onrush,
> And there, lifts, curling in spume,
>   Unlocks, drops from that hold
> Over and shoreward. The beach receives it,
>   A whitening line, collapsing
> Powdering-off down its broken length;
>   Then, curded, shallow, heavy
> With clustering bubbles, it nears
>   In a slow sheet that must climb

Relinquishing its power, upward
    Across tilted sand. Unravelled now
And the shore, under its lucid pane,
    Clear to the sight, it is spent:
The sun rocks there, as the netted ripple
    Into whose skeins the motion threads it
Glances athwart a bed, honey-combed
    By heaving stones. Neither survives the instant
But is caught back, and leaves, like the after-image
    Released from the floor of a now different mind,
A quick gold, dyeing the uncovering beach
    With sunglaze. That which we were,
Confronted by all that we are not,
    Grasps in subservience its replenishment.

The greater part of this is devoted to that characteristically sustained, careful, exact, sensitive description which is so justly admired. Only in the last five lines does the submerged simile make itself felt: the sea's encounter with the beach is an image of the process of change in the mind. We may accept the beauty and appropriateness of the comparison. But do we infer from it that Tomlinson believes, in Romantic fashion, that the structure of the universe mirrors that of the mind (or *vice versa*)? That would seem to be going too far: his similes are never given the slightest metaphyscial support. Is he, then, simply imposing some chance perception of similitude on the universe of things? Perhaps. But that sounds a trifle obtrusive and arbitrary when one considers the seriousness of his attitude towards natural objects, and of the reflections he makes upon them. The movement from perception to reflection is best seen as a response to an unspoken general injunction of this kind: 'You should record sensitively, and with answering attention, the phenomena of the world; and the reflections which arise from them should be such as will be spiritually edifying.' Yet, in the nature of Tomlinson's world, there is no binding reason why one should behave in this way, apart from a disposition to do so. The mind and the world of things remain of unlike substance, however tightly their threads may be woven together. And this too is evident from 'The Atlantic'. For what reflections should one have on the earlier part of the poem, what similes for the mental life might one construct upon it? When we read of the 'whitening line, collapsing, / Powdering-off down its broken length', could we or should we see this as a metaphor for mental process? And what of 'curded, shallow, heavy / With clustering bubbles'? Possibly. But only by doubtful inference; and the fact that Tomlinson leaves these things without comment suggests that we should do so too. It was not the poem he wrote, and it would not be typical of him. If it existed, such a poem would indeed intrude on the natural world in a way that he would find offensive, and it might even seem frivolous and superficial if it suggested that the world is there to provide us with a stock of metaphors for mind, and that it can do so easily.

And so, without arrogance or assumption, Tomlinson strenuously exacts his nugget of spiritual illumination from a world that remains outside us. The strenuous fidelity, the spiritual residue, suggest Ruskin as a forebear, which he is: Ruskin 'is one of the texts that [Marianne Moore] and I had in common . . . he was the writer of whom we spoke most. "He knew everything, didn't he!" she said.'[16]

III

Tomlinson's complaint about the Movement poets, about their want of awareness of 'the mystery bodied over against them in the created universe' points to what he himself is trying to achieve. That fine poem 'Descartes and the Stove', from *The Way of a World*, can be seen as a powerful, indirect argument for such awareness. A beautiful exactitude, set against the doubting Cartesian mind, achieves the status, as Jonathan Raban says, of 'an exquisite tribute to the solidity of the real':[17]

>   The foot-print
>   He had left on entering, had turned
>   To a firm dull gloss, and the chill
>   Lined it with a fur of frost. Now
> The last blaze of day was changing
>   All white to yellow, filling
> With bluish shade the slots and spoors
>   Where, once again, badger and fox would wind
> Through the phosphorescence

The intensity of the impressions is offered as a refutation of doubt as to the evidence of the senses, according to the logic, though not the manner, of Johnson on Berkeley. Of course, for Descartes, doubt was a method for discovering the true essences of things. It was not a dogma. He did not end by doubting the physical world: he entertained doubt as a means of arriving at certainty – the first certainty being that he could not doubt that he was thinking. But Tomlinson's poem has another target: the Cartesian dualism of mind and the physical (including the body):

> The great mind
> Sat with his back to the unreasoning wind
> And doubted, doubted at his   ear
> The patter of ash and, beyond, the snow-bound farms,
> Flora of flame and iron contingency
> And the moist reciprocation of his palms.

The last line may be intended primarily to quell doubt, but it also suggests that dualism is absurd. It is not, perhaps, an argument Descartes would take seriously – though the use of such physical states in arguments against dualism is not philosophically vacuous, as the example of phenomenology shows. Yet even while it makes its tribute to the world of sense, and shows Descartes as a physical being reacting to the physical world around, the poem, in its very method of recording first the physical, then the activities of mind, enacts a separation which its concluding statement would seek to deny. The poem is exemplary in the way that it conforms to the frequent Tomlinson pattern of movement from the physical to the mental, in the crucial case of a reflection on the relations of mind and body.

The self as embodied is a frequent theme of Tomlinson's, nowhere more finely treated than in the first poem in *The Way of a World*, 'Swimming Chenango Lake'. This begins with a luminous description of the autumnal appearance of the water:

> There is a geometry of water, for this
> Squares off the clouds' redundancies

> And sets them floating in a nether atmosphere
> All angles and elongations: every tree
> Appears a cypress as its stretches there
> And every bush that shows the season,
> A shaft of fire.

But the swimmer plunges, 'and now / Body must recall the eye to its independence / As he scissors the waterscape apart / And sways it to tatters.' The swimmer's relationship with the water is a metaphor for the relationship between the world, and the self conceived as embodied:

> He reaches in-and-through to that space
> The body is heir to, making a where
> In water, a possession to be relinquished
> Willingly at each stroke. The image he has torn
> Flows-to behind him, healing itself,
> Lifting and lengthening, splayed like the feathers
> Down an immense wing whose darkening spread
> Shadows his solitariness.

Here the self enters into a mutually supportive transaction with the material world, one that damages neither partner. The self has to find 'a where' in that world, perpetually; but the world, though it accedes to that pressure, always heals itself into its prior and essential separateness:

> Human, he fronts it and, human, he draws back
> From the interior cold, the mercilessness
> That yet shows a kind of mercy sustaining him.

The relationship is delicately poised. But the body, for Tomlinson, is not the site of desire and appetite, but the frontier where the encounter with the world occurs: an extension of the sensorium, an appropriate membrane for the metting with a world that presents itself as sense-data, and, of course, for finding 'a where' there. The body leaves the mind untouched, except in that it elicits reflection, as in this poem. And so it also leaves the divorce between mind and world untouched: it seems more an agent of the mind than part of a body-mind.

It is not surprising to find that this encounter should recall the first man:

> alone, he is unnamed
> By this baptism, where only Chenango bears a name
> In a lost language he begins to construe –
> A speech of densities and derisions, of half-
> Replies to questions his body must frame

The 'lost language' of the American Indians, like the Adamic language, fits word and thing together, and, in so doing, mirrors the encounter in which the thing is known. It is a 'speech of densities' because it represents the physical world, and of 'derisions' because the physical world only half-submits to the human pressure for 'a where', just as it provides only 'half-replies.' The Tomlinson poem itself corresponds to this Adamic language, and to this half-reply: the tentative, exploratory, sensitive rendering of experience, always remembering the resistance and otherness of the world, as in this poem's final glance at the water: 'The going-elsewhere of ripples incessantly shaping.'

In a poem called 'Adam' we learn that finding a language like that of Eden is a matter of allowing things to speak through words:

> We tell them over, surround them
> In a world of sounds, and they are heard
> Not drowned in them

Nevertheless, this pure apprehension contains its quota of our own being: 'We bring / To a kind of birth all we can name / And, named, it echoes in us our being.' Once again we have to accept that the world, as truly apprehended, mirrors our selves as truly apprehending, without being given any reason why this should be so. And, as so often in the post-Romantic tradition, the pure perception which contains this sense of 'echo' is prior to language while at the same time its founding moment.

Another poem from *The Way of a World*, 'The Chances of Rhyme', alludes to Adam and Eden in the context of a discussion of art. Here Tomlinson rejects errors to either side of the difficult encounter of man and world, the one kind of encounter which can yield enduring significance: 'Why should we speak / Of art, of life, as if the one were all form / And the other all Sturm-und-Drang?' The implication being that art may mould itself organically to the form of life, and life may yield an

orderly meaning. This is a result which can only arise out of that
strenuous process of discovery which so many of the poems seek to
exemplify. And in this one Tomlinson uses the metaphor of the use of
rhyme to convey the message:

> The chances of rhyme are like the chances of meeting –
> In the finding fortuitous, but once found, binding:
> They say, they signify and they succeed, where to succeed
> Means not success, but a way forward

The conclusive, 'binding' effect of rhyme is analogous to the effect of
the discovery of orderly meaning. The realm of chance, on the other
hand, is the chaos (as it may first appear) of the world of phenomena: a
feminine chaos, as the metaphor of marriage makes clear. The conclusive
effect of rhyme, however, like the discovery of meaning, is a precarious
moment in a constant struggle:

> immersion, conversion – of inert
> Mass, that is, into energies to combat confusion.
> Let rhyme be my conclusion.

'Inert / Mass' is significantly charged with associations of stubborn
resistance. And this means the resistance both of language and the world
of things. In all of this one may discern a thoroughly secularized and
highly tentative version of that Romantic sleight-of-hand I discerned in
Wordsworth and Coleridge, where the poet seeks unconvincingly to give
the impression that transcendent meaning has emerged from an encounter with Nature where Nature's resistance must also be recorded.

7

TED HUGHES

I

Hughes is a visionary empiricist in his best-known poems, a poet of what I have called 'the empiricist moment'. Capturing the object was Hughes's earliest aim. The intense realizing of things and animals is always striking and ingenious, but is often given no consistency within the poem, which tends to become a series of isolated transcriptions of moments of perception:

> The wind flung a magpie away and a black-
> Back gull bent like an iron bar slowly. The house
> Rang like some fine green goblet in the note
> That any second would shatter it.
>
> ('Wind')[1]

But at other times a train of metaphors will be subdued to Hughes's purpose of capturing and distilling the life of what he is describing. Thus, in 'Hawk Roosting', all the imagery suggests control, a quality Hughes often seems to value highly. He almost always chooses beasts who share 'bullet and automatic / Purpose' with the thrush ('Thrushes').[2] 'Control' is not far removed from 'capturing'. The accent is always on the individual poet's solitary but powerful imagination, reconstructing the external world by means of striking and ingenious figures, but able to find there no meaning save the reflection of the poet's own activity.

As Martin Dodsworth says, 'most of Hughes's poems' embody 'funda-mentally isolated experience'.[3] This metaphorical style, and its deploy-ment in a fashion which stresses isolation, have been very influential on British and Irish poetry.

Of course, for all the talk of 'accuracy' and 'perception', no poet succeeds in creating descriptions to which one could definitively attach the word 'objective'. As we have seen, Hughes's intensive figures and obsession with control help to constitute his own characteristic form of prejudice. But perhaps the most interesting deviation from 'objectivity' is to be found in the character of Hughes's figurative language. For although he speaks as if he defers to Nature, he frequently converts the natural into the mechanical or industrial. This might not seem very likely, so perhaps a brief catalogue can be excused: the Jaguar is seen 'hurrying enraged / Through prison darkness after the drills of his eyes / On a short fierce fuse'. In 'October Dawn' the ice puts 'plate and rivet on pond and brook; / Then tons of chain and massive lock'. In 'Mayday on Holderness' the speaker looks 'down into the decomposition of leaves – / The furnace door whirling with larvae', while in 'November' he stays 'on under the welding cold ... In the drilling rain'. We have already mentioned the 'bullet and automatic / Purpose' of 'Thrushes', but not the fact that they are 'more coiled steel than living', nor that they are 'Triggered', 'streamlined' and possess 'efficiency'. Crow, too, is mecha-nical: 'his head, trapsprung, stabbed' ('Crow Tyrannosaurus'). In *Season Songs* the swifts are a 'shrapnel-scatter' ('Swifts') and in 'Earth-numb' from *Moortown* the salmon possesses an 'electrocuting malice'.

The ambivalence of Hughes's response to Nature is clear from any sensitive reading. There is a partial identification with an impersonal ruthlessness which denies the finer feelings and, as we shall see, impli-citly, and sometimes explicitly, chastises the 'feminine'. Hughes's very vitalism, with its roots in Romantic organicism, expresses itself in terms of the imagery of machines. In this he shows himself to stand in a line of descent that runs from Hardy through the poets of the First World War and certain areas of the work of D. H. Lawrence. There is less ambiva-lence about this in Hughes's early work than in that of his mentors; but it may be seen in the way the speaker often experiences mechanically conceived natural forces as a threat (staying under 'the drilling rain'). One should not over-emphasize this. The chief tone is one of admiring delight: if the thrushes are 'automatic', it is nevertheless by virtue of this fact that they achieve comparison with Mozart. It is really in *Crow* that Hughes begins to look critically at his own stance and at its historical context.[4] And then it is in terms of an incipient critique of the relationship between the sexes in modern industrial society. This critique is the true subject of *Gaudete*.[5]

II

'She is Isis, mother of the gods, Graves' White Goddess.' Thus Keith Sagar identifies the sick woman, 'tangled in the skins of wolves', who appears in the Prologue to *Gaudete*.[6] The identification may have surprised not a few of Sagar's readers, and the same may be true of his attempt to show that *Gaudete* as a whole is a highly personal and lively rehearsal of aspects of the White Goddess myth, to which Graves's book is a useful key. Can this be the Hughes of the 'sulking bitches' and *Crow*? Yet Sagar makes a good case, which nobody can disbelieve after reading Stuart Hirschberg's recent, very thorough book, *Myth in the Poetry of Ted Hughes*.[7] Nor can anyone now believe that Hughes's interest in the occult is new, nor that it was ever superficial.

What emerges from these studies is Hughes's passionate concern with what he sees as the alienation of male and female from each other. But it is possible to discern a pattern of development in Hughes's treatment of this theme without invoking Jung or Graves too much. This is what I shall attempt to do here. What one discovers is the importance of this theme, from the earliest poems; and a sense of deliberate progression reminiscent of that one gains from the work of Gunn.

There is much misogyny in Hughes's earlier writings. It is in misogyny that the misanthrope of 'Soliloquy of a Misanthrope' (from *The Hawk in the Rain*) finds the best reason for welcoming death:

> But I shall thank God thrice heartily
> To be lying beside women who grimace
> Under the commitments of their flesh,
> And not out of spite or vanity.

There is a startling savagery in the sexual ambiguity of this, suggesting that women especially are ready to sacrifice even the power of the Life-Force for perverted social ends, evading the power of sexuality for petty self-aggrandisement. In *The Hawk in the Rain* the Life-Force is masculine. In 'Macaw and little Miss' the girl

> lies under every full moon,
> The spun glass of her body bared and so gleam-still
> Her brimming eyes do not tremble or spill
> The dream where the warrior comes, lightning and iron,
> Smashing and burning and rending towards her loin.

The excitement at violent, phallic power has its corollary in an un-qualified admiration for masculine force in general. Such feelings consort well with a traditional kind of male distrust of women, and many of the old stereotypes make their appearance in Hughes's work. We know that Hughes was already fascinated by the White Goddess.[8] And she may seem, at times, destructive. As Graves says: 'The poet is in love with the White Goddess, with Truth: his heart breaks with longing and love for her. She is the Flower-goddess Olwen or Blodeuwedd; but she is also Blodeuwedd the Owl, lamp-eyed, hooting dismally, with her foul nest in the hollow of a dead tree, or Circe the pitiless falcon, or Lamia with her flickering tongue.'[9] Hughes may intend some such idea, but there is not much sense of 'longing and love' in his work until now. He is much nastier than Graves gives grounds for being. The Goddess is, indeed, terrifying, because amoral, and because she may withdraw love and inspiration from the poet. But Graves does not approve the contempt Hughes shows: it is to those who treat her with contempt that the Goddess reveals only her terrifying visage, according to Graves.[10]

   Even so, *The Hawk in the Rain* offers a hint of the ambiguous love-hate which Hughes feels towards the feminine; his version, in fact, of what should have been, in Graves's terms, love-fear. In 'Song' the more positive side of this comes through:

> O lady, consider when I shall have lost you ...
> And my head, worn out with love, at rest
> In my hands, and my hands full of dust,
> O my lady.

The attitude to women remains markedly negative right up to the time, however, when *Gaudete* was written. Hughes's horrified fascination is well represented by 'Fragment of an ancient tablet', from *Crow*:

Above – many a painful frown.
Below – the ticking bomb of the future.

Above – her perfect teeth, with the hint of a fang at the corner.
Below – the millstones of two worlds.

Above – a word and a sigh.
Below – gouts of blood and babies.

Over the years Hughes also gradually distils a concentrated version of the Life-Force. He had begun, of course, with the various animals and birds. But already, in *Lupercal*, a stoat, caught and nailed to the door, re-emerges 'thirsting, in far Asia, in Brixton' ('Strawberry Hill'). It is a universal principle. This stoat is, so to speak, a kind of Crow.

In *Wodwo* this movement towards a simple, generalized myth is accelerated.[11] Hughes tries to define the primeval force in terms that transcend the use of animals merely. Thus in 'Theology' we have the first of Hughes's poems about Adam and Eve and the serpent. In 'Gog' that ancient mythical giant is the vital force. And the 'wodwo' of the book's title is another mythical creature, half beast and half man. The culmination of this tendency towards a universal myth is, of course, *Crow*, the hero of which is only occasionally reminiscent of an empirical bird. It is very much the Life-Force in all the squalor, ruthlessness, power and vitality Hughes had come to attribute to it. And it is, of course, very male: a fact sufficiently emphasized by Leonard Baskin's familiar design for the dustjacket.

Now it could be claimed that Hughes is in fact as uncomplimentary to this male principle as he is to the female. But such is not the case. Although Crow is to be found 'spraddled head-down in the beach-garbage, guzzling a dropped ice-cream', while other birds partake of the sublime, there is clearly a large quota of admiration of Crow's brutal honesty. Automatic though Crow's purpose can be ('But his eye saw a grub. And his head, trapsprung, stabbed': 'Crow Tyrannosaurus') we are well aware that this is the same poet who complimented Mozart's mind

on sharing 'bullet and automatic / Purpose' with the thrush while des-
pising the petty art of those who are too conscious.

References to the female are relatively few. But in a curious way the
fear and loathing Hughes evinces in them add up to a kind of back-
handed compliment. This is significant. At the end of 'Logos' in *Wodwo*,
we learn that 'God is a good fellow, but His mother's against Him'.
Since it is the ruthless powers of Nature which conspire to ruin God's
fine purposes, it is clear that God's mother is the principle of the
Life-Force conceived of as female. This suggestion of female power is to
be expanded in *Crow*. In 'Song for a phallus' Crow gives his own version
of the Oedipus story. 'The way Crow tells the story Oedipus attempts
matricide as well as patricide because the mother is ultimately responsi-
ble for the horror of existence.'[12]

> He split his Mammy like a melon
> He was drenched with gore
> He found himself curled up inside
> As if he had never been bore
>   Mamma Mamma

Here the mother fulfils exactly the same all-inclusive function as the
serpent in 'Theology', which becomes a dark intestine containing the
whole world. In 'Song for a phallus' the mother assumes some of these
connotations of sexuality and devouring greed, but adds to these her
own: that of the womb.

It is important to note that violence against the mother only serves to
stress dependence on her. The violence – that of the assertive but
discomfited male – is shown to be humiliatingly futile.

Crow shows the beginning of self-analysis in Hughes, by which I
mean that he begins to analyse and place some masculine attitudes
which are congruent with those to be found in his earlier work:

> There was a person
> Could not get rid of his mother
> As if he were her topmost twig.
> So he pounded and hacked at her
> With numbers and equations and laws
> Which he invented and called truth.

He investigated, incriminated
And penalised her, like Tolstoy,
Forbidding, screaming and condemning,
Going for her with a knife,
Obliterating her with disgusts
Bulldozers and detergents
Requisitions and central heating
Rifles and whisky and bored sleep.

('Revenge fable')

This agrees with Graves's analysis of masculine religions, and in particular Judaeo-Christianity, which are founded in fear of the feminine, and
which are supposed to have suppressed the cult of the Magna Mater.
One expression of the state of mind encouraged by patriarchal religion is
to be found in the desecration of nature; but rationalism, rape and
marriage laws are others.

It is a short step from this poem, which is a piece of cultural analysis,
to a poem which takes patriarchal error as its main theme. *Gaudete* is
such a poem; and it also contains, in the songs of the resurrected 'Lumb'
at the end of the book, poems which evince a large element of the confessional, and which implicate their author in patriarchal error, while
expressing his joyful submission to the principle against which he has
fought so long and so joylessly. The way out lies in an accommodation
with the feminine.

Crow can be seen as a descent into hell, or, in alchemical parlance,
Melancholy, which is a necessary prelude to resurrection, or the finding of the philosopher's stone. Hughes, with his interest in Jung and
alchemy, must have been pleased to reflect that the 'melancholy' or black
phase of the alchemical amalgam was known as the 'head of the raven'.[13]
I should add that he may have come across a reference specifically to a
crow as symbol of the dark stage in Jung's *Alchemical Studies*:

My soul and spirit fast are sinking,
And leave a poison, black and stinking.
To a black crow am I akin,
Such be the wages of all sin.[14]

In *Gaudete* Hughes feels he has found the philosopher's stone of spiritual
renewal, as the title implies. The right relationship with the feminine,

so necessary for this, can be discerned in the symbol of the alchemical union of opposites necessary for the Great Work. The opposites are, chemically, Sulphur and Mercury. But the symbols for them are legion: Fire and Water, Eagle and Serpent, Sun and Moon, King and Queen, Bride and Groom.[15] The union of these opposites, necessary to create the philosopher's stone, is called, in alchemical parlance, a 'Marriage', as in Blake's *The Marriage of Heaven and Hell*, a work which draws on the alchemical tradition. Hirschberg is right to see in the poem 'Bride and groom lie hidden for three days', from *Cave Birds*, an allusion to the alchemical marriage.[16] It is significant that this celebratory poem, in which male and female 'bring each other to perfection', is so near the sequence's conclusion, marked by a poem called 'The risen'. The soul has to go through the black or melancholy stage, and through a union of opposites, in order to be reborn. A clear allusion to the black part of this process can be seen in a poem near the end of *Adam and the Sacred Nine:* 'The Crow came to Adam':

> Who has understood the Crow's love-whisper?
> Or the Crow's news?
>
> Adam woke.[17]

The stage of the Crow is necessary to enlightenment.

The point to stress in all this is not the idea of the alchemical opposites in general, but the specific conception of these opposites as masculine and feminine, and as having to go through a black stage before renewal. *Gaudete* is also a work on these themes.

The many links in symbolism between *Gaudete* and *The White Goddess* have been discussed in detail by Sagar and Hirschberg. I shall rather, in pursuing my theme, concentrate on the distinctive feel of the book, and the way that its meaning becomes clearer when read in conjunction with Hughes's earlier work.

After the Prologue one very quickly comes upon Major Hagen, the kind of character who in an earlier book might have been something of a hero:

> A perfunctory campaign leatheriness.
> A frontal Viking weatherproof

Drained of the vanities, pickled in mess-alcohol and smoked dark.
Anaesthetised
For ultimate cancellations
By the scathing alums of King's regulations,
The petrifying nitrates of garrison caste.[18]

We learn of the 'artillery target-watching poise of his limbs' and that his underlip 'Is not moved / Forty generations from the freezing salt and the longships'. The Major himself is reminiscent of 'The Retired Colonel' in *Lupercal*, 'five or six wars / Stiffened in his reddened neck'. The reference to ruthlessness is prolonged in 'the iron arteries of Calvin', The 'artillery target-watching poise' is like the 'bullet and automatic purpose' of the thrushes.

But in *Gaudete* it is Hagen who annihilates the hopefully Dionysian oak-version of Lumb (that is to say, the Reverend Lumb, a vicar transformed into an heroic fertility god with significant overtones of the organic) and the gun with which he does the deed is described in significantly sexual terms:

Hagen, leaning in the window-frame,
Cheekbone snug to the glossed walnut, introduces his first
    love to the panorama of his marriage and retirement.
The Mannlicher . 318
Regards Lumb's distant skull dutifully, with perfectly
    tooled and adjusted concentration.
Germanic precision, slender goddess
Of Hagen's devotions
And the unfailing bride
Of his ecstacies in the primal paradise.[19]

These lines depict the machine-like manliness of Hagen in a relationship with his gun which is a parody of the 'true marriage' of the sexes in which Hughes now believes. Furthermore, Hagen's 'bride' can be seen as a mechanical and destructive symbol of the phallus, in which case his most binding attachment is to a brutalized form of his own sexuality.

The oak-changeling, Lumb, is an opposed figure, not so much because he reveals that 'Christianity depends on women' and 'all those other religions, too, depend on women', in Old Smayle's words.[20] More important is the related fact that the very quality of his experience is of openness, of a frightening sensitivity:

> He sees the grass
> And feels the wind pulse over his skin.
> He feels the hill he stands on, hunched, swelling,
> Piling through him, complete and permanent with stone,
> Filling his skull, squeezing his thoughts out from his eyes
> To fritter away across surfaces.[21]

This openness and closeness to nature is a correlative of his ability to fascinate and inflame women. Though not fully human he is able to give vent to and elicit the repressed Dionysian in those who, for opposed reasons, might also be said to be not fully human.

When the changeling Lumb is killed, the original Nicholas Lumb reappears 'in the West of Ireland, where he roams about composing hymns and psalms to a nameless female deity'.[22] Lumb is reborn having been made whole: the two opposed parts of his personality, the Apollonian and the Dionysian, have been reconciled. And these two categories correspond to masculine and feminine. Furthermore he has understood that it is the Goddess he must thank for this. She it is who brings inspiration and renewal: 'I let in again – / As if for the first time – / The untouched joy'; 'So you have come and gone again / With my skin'.[23] It is because of a purifying death of his old self that this has become possible: hence the title of the book, *Gaudete*, a word which appears only once within it, where it is the solitary inscription on a gravestone which Maud stops at when walking in a graveyard.

A graveyard is also mentioned in the songs of the resurrected 'Lumb':

> Waving goodbye, from your banked hospital bed,
> Waving, weeping, smiling, flushed
> It happened
> You knocked the world off, like a flower-vase.
>
> It was the third time. And it smashed.
>
> I turned
> I bowed
> In the morgue I kissed

Your temple's refrigerated glazed
As rained-on graveyard marble, my
Lips queasy, heart non-existent[24]

The reference to Sylvia Plath's suicide is made clear by 'It was the third
time': as she herself wrote in 'Lady Lazarus', 'This is Number Three'. It
seems that Plath, and possibly other actual women, and not just an
abstract white goddess, is referred to in many of the songs to the 'female
deity'. Plath's grave in Heptonstall churchyard had figured in *Wodwo*:

> Black village of gravestones.
> The hill's collapsed skull
> Whose dreams die back
> Where they were born
>
> ('Heptonstall')

In *Remains of Elmet* 'Heptonstall Cemetry' refers to names on tombstones,
including 'Sylvia'.[25] *Gaudete* is, in part, a book about how Hughes feels
that he has gathered some insight and, in the end, joy out of tragic
experiences. The gravestone belongs, with *Crow*, to the melancholy or
black phase; it was equally necessary, and its lesson is equally one of
reconciliation between the sexes.

What helps one to believe that an important change may have
occurred in Hughes's work is the texture of these songs themselves.
They are the first of his poems to address or speak of an Other on the
implied basis of relationship, rather than describing or controlling or
'capturing' objects or animals:

> Once I said lightly
> Even if the worst happens
> We can't fall off the earth.
>
> And again I said
> No matter what fire cooks us
> We shall be still in the pan together.
>
> And words twice as stupid.
> Truly hell heard me.

She fell into the earth
And I was devoured.[26]

Many of the statements in the songs have to be understood as referring
to a passionate private relationship. They form part of the tradition of
love lyric. Indeed, bringing with them Hughes's descriptive powers and
laconic but strong phrasing, they represent something new in this
tradition in Britain. Equally, they are an advance on Hughes's work
hitherto. There was always something too 'one-dimensional' about
Hughes's brilliantly descriptive earlier work: to describe, especially in
the most startling 'kennings', is to display mastery. The new poems
emerge from a more open and chastened state of mind.

And in analysis they can be seen as more complex; a fundamentally
lyric mode, of passionate, singing statement and address, controls clus-
ters of images related to the more general idea of the Goddess, and
others related to actual private experience. The ideas may remain general, or may be conveyed in imagery which displays all of Hughes's
habitual powers of description ('Your Oak / A glare / / Of black upward
lightning'.[27] This synthesis of Goddess ideas with personal address and
vivid empiricals makes for the kind of complexity which has always
provided the excitement and appeal of poetry, but which seems to be ill
understood in the past decade or so by reviewers who give the impression that vivid description is the touchstone of good writing. And even
so astute and irreverent a critic as David Trotter, who rejects the law of
description, can refer to *Gaudete* as 'saccharine', without feeling the need
to explain the criticism: Hughes has offended too starkly against the
modern idolatry of 'anti-pathos', as Trotter describes it, sometimes with
irony but never with apostasy.

Hughes provides the example of a poet whose practice has changed
radically in conjunction with his notions about gender: the disavowal of
the ideology of masculine control and ruthless mechanical-bestial energy
has consorted with a shedding of techniques which suggest the opera-
tions of an isolated, self-consciously ingenious and domineering mind.
Some of the poems in *Moortown* suggest the continuation of this progress, some do not. It will be interesting to see what direction is
followed by any new, major work.

8

SYLVIA PLATH

Sylvia Plath has more things to do in her poems than concentrate on objects. Yet when she deals with them – and that is often – she attempts to convey a vivid sense of their appearance. At the same time the metaphors she chooses are often imbued with exotic or bizarre associations derived from the symbolic drama she uses to interpret her experience. Yet one does not feel that objects are being manipulated in order to display the poet's ingenuity or facility. Rather, one assents to the gravity the poet accords to the drama she describes and accepts that objects have a subordinate, though important, supporting role. Neverthelesss, it seems to me that some subsequent poets, including Craig Raine, have been greatly influenced by her at the level of her handling of objects: in accepting an arbitrary-seeming exoticism for the vehicles of their metaphors (without suffering from the psychological causes of that exoticism); in conveying a marked sense of alienation; and in dealing boldly with domestic items.

But one aspect belongs to Plath alone: she makes herself an object. And the way in which she does this is conditioned by her sense of herself as an object for the male. Most readers of Plath are familiar with the schizoid detachment from the body expressed in 'Cut':

> What a thrill –
> My thumb instead of an onion.
> The top quite gone
> Except for a sort of hinge

> Of skin,
> A flap like a hat,
> Dead white.
> Then that red plush.[1]

This is only the most striking example of such detachment. In other cases it is experienced as being watched and found wanting:

> The sheep know where they are,
> Browsing in their dirty wool-clouds,
> Gray as the weather.
> The black slots of their pupils take me in.
> It is like being mailed into space,
> A thin silly messaage.
>
>   ("Wuthering Heights")

And some poems bring together the sense of the body as object and the sense of being watched as part of the response to the male:

> A living doll, everywhere you look.
> It can sew, it can cook,
>
> It can talk, talk, talk.
>
> It works, there is nothing wrong with it.
> You have a hole, it's a poultice.
> You have an eye, it's an image.
> My boy, it's your last resort.
> Will you marry it, marry it, marry it.
>
>   ("The Applicant")

Or, more succinctly in 'Lady Lazarus':

> So, so, Herr Doktor.
> So, Herr Enemy.
>
> I am your opus,
> I am your valuable,
> The pure gold baby
>
> That melts to a shriek.

But the persona is constantly threatening to reverse the positions in this power-relationship: Lady Lazarus ends with the threat, 'Out of the ash / I rise with my red hair / And I eat men like air.' A poem written about the same time, 'Purdah', exploits even more clearly the piquant contrast between the woman's apparent powerlessness and her intended role as a vengeful figure akin to Clytemnestra:

> I shall unloose –
> From the small jeweled
> Doll he guards like a heart –
>
> The lioness,
> The shriek in the bath,
> The cloak of holes.

The proximity of the contrasting images suggests that the two roles for the woman are closely related: that there is a natural resentment created in the first role, and a natural progression towards the second; and further that, although the lioness is more ostensibly threatening than the doll, the latter is also inhuman and sinister. And both roles are imposed by the male. His attempts to belittle and reify the speaker are seen as equivalent to a desire to kill her. The two types of the male in 'Death & Co' – the hard man and the weak Don Juan – both treat the woman as an object: for the former she is 'red meat'; for the latter, a prop to weak narcissism: 'Bastard / Masturbating a glitter, / He wants to be loved.' It is her death they foster, and may well encompass:

> I do not stir.
> The frost makes a flower,
> The dew makes a star,
> The dead bell,
> The dead bell,
>
> Somebody's done for.

This ending is dense with ambiguities. The speaker does not stir because she is being cautious, like a mouse hiding from a cat. Or she does not stir because she feels disinclined to respond. Or because she is nearly dead. Or because she is dead already, in which case the bell is for her.

But if she is not dead, the bell suggests, combined with the black humour of the last line, that 'Death & Co' are a danger to all women. All of these meanings, as well as the pellucid and tense evocation of a sinister stillness, contribute to the unparaphrasable effect of this ending.

For ambivalent reasons the speaker conforms to the male intention that she should die. By doing so she can think of herself as returning to her dead father: 'Father, this thick air is murderous. / I would breathe water' ('Full Fathom Five'). The dead father is the only case of the male as 'good object': an original point of acceptance and wholeness, unsullied by time – even by the time in which the living father made her suffer. By returning to the dead father she is also rejecting imitations ('The vampire who said he was you'–'Daddy') and gaining her revenge on the living male.

But in accepting the idea that she should die she is also acceding to the male's view of her as close to an object. That is why she adopts this view as her own and sees herself as the male, she believes, sees her. To the extent that she looks at objects and herself in the same detached and alienated way, she believes herself to be adopting some of the features of a masculine view of the world. But when the project ends, in death, objects will cease to be unrelated or threatening: she will dissolve into an undifferentiated unity, a unity which will confer a power withheld from her in the male-dominated, post-pubertal world. Hence the triumphal tone of her intimations of suicide:

> And now I
> Foam to wheat, a glitter of seas.
> The child's cry
>
> Melts in the wall.
> And I
> Am the arrow,
>
> The dew that flies
> Suicidal, at one with the drive
> Into the red
>
> Eye, the cauldron of morning.

                                                                    ('Ariel')

The end of 'Fever 103°' is similar: '(My selves dissolving, old whore petticoats) – / To Paradise'. This plenitude, both original and post-mortem, certainly belongs to the realm of what Lacan would call the Imaginary: the union with the dead father representing the woman's assumption of the phallus. This reading is supported by the references to orgasm which constitute a layer of meaning in each of these passages: the ecstacy is not experienced as growing out of a relationship with the man. It is something the speaker enjoys as celebration of herself and her power. In 'Fever 103°', although she addresses her 'Darling' in a frankly sexual manner, it is only to remark that 'I am too pure for you or anyone. / Your body / Hurts me as the world hurts God.' Passion and ecstacy are described as states of her own being, a pure, virginal being, divesting itself of entanglements with the male and the male-dominated world. This self-contained ecstacy has already assumed power over the phallus. The next step is to go forever beyond a world where the structure of relationships between man and woman means only a living death to her.

But for the time being there are poems to write, poems which still inhabit that world. There is an implicit identification of the poetry with the substance of the speaker's life: understandable in view of the way the symbolic dramas enacted in them, taken together, are obviously intended to exhibit in full the structures which give shape to that life. Death, which will quell the conflicts, will also stop the poetry. The plausible link between language and the entrapment of her life is forged by Plath herself in the poem 'Words', written a few days before her death. But it is not a link whose precise nature is easy to grasp:

> Axes
> After whose stroke the wood rings,
> And the echoes!
> Echoes traveling
> Of from the center like horses.
>
> The sap
> Wells like tears, like the
> Water striving
> To re-establish its mirror
> Over the rock

That drops and turns,
A white skull,
Eaten by weedy greens.
Years later I
Encounter them on the road –

Words dry and riderless,
The indefatigable hoof-taps.
While
From the bottom of the pool, fixed stars
Govern a life.

The first thing this poem does is to focus on the moment of creation of meaning, the moment the axe cleaves the living wood. Meaning is created in a moment of destruction of wholeness, recalling Lacan's account of how entry into the Symbolic, and thus into language, is conditioned by the castration complex. If this recourse to psychoanalysis seems dubious, it may be worth reflecting yet again on the traumatic relationships with father and lovers which provide so much of the substance and detail of Plath's poetry. In this particular case it is important to note that the creation of meaning in the first stanza seems to have occurred at one particular point in past time. This becomes clearer at the end of the third stanza: 'Years later I / Encounter them on the road / / Words dry and riderless.' The poem refers not to moments in the constant creation of meaning, but to the founding moment of that creation in the past. From this emanate the words: their status as 'echoes' makes them seem tenuous compared to the violent act which transmitted them. And there is no suggestion that they point to anything but that act. When the speaker encounters them again they are 'dry and riderless': the description reinforces the message that their true home is the axe in the moist sap of the wood. And it also implies that they are disconnected from life and from any clear purpose. But purpose there is of a kind: the predestinating influence of the fixed stars which ordain everything. The stars, themselves part of nature, are at the bottom of the pool (one can imagine them reflected there), and thus align themselves with moisture, 'sap' and life, as opposed to the dryness of words. But life itself is cruelly indifferent, identical with an amoral

Necessity: it has caused the original trauma and everything that flowed from it.

The poem does not imply that 'language is male', however. The most that can be directly inferred from this poem is that language arises out of some primordial act of destruction or desecration that threatens the self. If one accepts my assimilation of this event to Lacan's description of the relation between castration and the entry into language, one may say that Plath is recording some kind of apprehension of these events. Yet it is not, of course, proven that she has conceptualized them in any way, let alone in something like Lacan's. But it seems reasonable to say that 'Words' has the effect of including language, along with the objects, actions and events of life, in the category of entities that have been alienated from the speaker through the agency of the father. And other poems indicate that the male sex in general continues this agency. Nevertheless, the determinism of the stars dictates her acquiescence in language, her entrapment in a medium which cannot speak her being authentically, but only point to the distant origin of a split in that being. We may extrapolate: language, like life, is marked by this split, and the poet has to negotiate her way through both, conscious that fullness of being cannot be expressed in either. She assumes the role of poet on these terms, sometimes with an air of triumph, as if to say: out of this very sense of imperfect being I shall create perfect poems. But the true sense of wholeness lies beyond time, sexuality and words.

The poems, being alive, even in such a world, have to work out their way between two conditions which often look alike: death (which brings plenitude) and a life so reified and alienated that it looks like death. (Let no one say that Plath is not a Romantic.) Poetry, lying between these terms, contains two levels (to make a convenient, if artificial distinction): at the bottom, approaching the world of living death, is the vivid, alienated recording of objects; at the top, approaching the world of death, and aware of its true meaning, is the level of symbolism. The symbolic level is explanatory: it explains why objects appear alien or threatening; and it explains why death is necessary. It also acts as the vehicle for the recording of sense impressions, which is why the distinction of levels is artificial.

For however much a Plath poem may sometimes seem to approximate to one of those virtuoso recordings to which we are so accustomed, it is

usually very far from doing so, especially in those poems that were
written after the publication of *The Colossus*. In 'The Moon and the Yew
Tree', for instance, we are invited by a number of signs to think of the
represented setting in concrete terms. The graveyard is 'Separated from
my house' by a row of headstones. The grass prickles the speaker's
ankles. The moon is 'White as a knuckle'. Clouds 'are flowering / . . .
over the face of the stars.' But equally we cannot ignore the weight of
symbolic meaning attached to the images. The moon is 'terribly upset'
and 'quiet / With the O-gape of complete despair'; 'She is not sweet like
Mary. / Her blue garments unloose small bats and owls.' The poem
mingles the sense of externality and internality as completely as some
Victorian symbolic landscape. The accent, however, is on the subjective
ordering: the statements in the poem can be convincingly interpreted as
a brief, consecutive unfolding of the salient points to be deduced from
the moon's being Plath's 'mother': that is to say that she identifies
herself, as a woman, with the cold, alienated despair she symbolizes by
the moon's attributes. Does this mean Plath's later poems are arbitrarily
subjective, to the extent that they conform to this model? By no means.
To take just this poem as an example, the image of the moon is used in
a number of her poems in a similar way and this use renders its
particular appearance in each more intelligible. One must also take
account of the traditional association of the moon with the feminine, and
of the symbolic drama of the relationship of man and woman which any
reader of Plath soon learns to bring in as a motivating force. The yew
tree which 'points up', whose message is 'blackness and silence', represents, in this poem, the inheritance of the father and his complete denial
of the speaker, as against the cold irrationality ('She is bald and wild')
which the speaker represents as a specifically feminine mode. Such an
approach to this poem is typical of the way in which many others may
be understood.

   A related argument against Plath sees her depiction of the relationship
between the sexes as pathological. Perhaps it is. Yet pathology may be
pedagogue to those who think themselves healthy. It should be firmly
asserted that what Plath describes has universal relevance, however
extreme her perceptions might appear. The idea of the objectification
and belittlement of women is of universal interest, and even the association of male dominance with fascism possesses a more disturbing *prima*

facie plausibility than many would like to think. All of this should be so obvious as to seem banal. But there is another argument, based on formal considerations rather than 'themes', which should help to deflect the imputation of malign subjectivism.

Plath's poems behave in an impersonal and formally complex manner. It is true, of course, that there are many statements in them containing first-person pronouns. But, overwhelmingly, these tend to be poetic entities. Instead of statements such as 'I feel despairing, insignificant, alienated, suicidal', one gets 'If I pay the roots of the heather / Too close attention, they will invite me / To whiten my bones among them.' ('Wuthering Heights') And the examples of 'Words' and 'The Moon and the Yew Tree' show how the poems create networks of images in linked, opposed and overlapping groups. 'Words', for instance, links sap, water on a rock and a pool, into a group meaning 'life'. It enriches this category, however, by likening the sap to 'tears' and the rock to a skull; and by putting the fixed stars at the bottom of the pool. 'Tears' is easy to read: the axes have wounded the tree; figuratively it denotes the speaker's grief. The skull and the stars are more difficult: they point respectively to some impulse towards death in the very substance of life, and to the fact that the sense of alienation in the present has been predestined by the very energies of nature which at first seemed to be totally opposed to the traumatic iron intrusion of the axe.

At a still more technical level, it should be noted that Plath is a highly rhetorical poet. She can hardly be described as a poet of direct pathos. She imparts a relatively impersonal air even to self–referential statements of the speaker. The poems are heavily coded. But she is very apt to reinforce the emotive implications of poems with rhetorical patterning. Consider, for instance, 'Kindness':

> Kindness glides about my house
> Dame Kindness, she is so nice!
> The blue and red jewels of her rings smoke
> In the windows, the mirrors
> Are filling with smiles.
>
> What is so real as the cry of a child?
> A rabbit's cry may be wilder
> But it has no soul.

Sugar can cure everything, so Kindness says.
Sugar is a necessary fluid,

Its crystals a little poultice.
O kindness, kindness
Sweetly picking up pieces!
My Japanese silks, desperate butterflies,
May be pinned any minute, anesthetized.

And here you come, with a cup of tea
Wreathed in steam.
The blood jet is poetry,
There is no stopping it.
You hand me two children, two roses.

Exclamation, rhetorical question, *invocatio*, repetition, all help to shape the sharp relief of the poem's tone. Against this background even the flatness of the last line takes on added force by contrast: here is no poet of compulsory cool: she chooses her moment for this. In addition, the rhetorical manner adds another element of variety to what is already a complex and variegated poem in terms of its imagery, and one which, characteristically, displays an interest in sound patterns, though less marked here than in many other poems – 'Daddy', for instance. Everything supports the view that these are offered as aesthetic, as well as symbolic, transformations of the experiences which, we infer, were probably their occasions.

The modern Anglo-American tradition is generally anxious to avoid the imputation of subjective emotionalism. In this it expresses a characteristic prejudice, but little else. So anxiously is this prejudice asserted that it leads to facile injustice in the occasional condemnation of poets such as Plath who attempt to represent subjectivity in an authentic manner while linking it to the collective condition. Further, she is a poet who employs art. It is true that she makes use of fairly traditional means in her poetry, though she uses them in adventurous ways. But that is not the same as treating the poem as the indulgence of emotion. Her work does not even fall foul of Modernist injunctions against personality. Its richness is a standing rebuke to objectivism – a rebuke rendered more cutting because one layer of her poetry is constituted by a vivid poetry of things. It is worth pondering the fact that she associates the detached view of things with a masculine perspective that has been imposed on her, and which tends to limit her, even though she proceeds to create a larger perspective within which this imposition is, it seems to her, explained. The link between male consciousness and the discourse of power over objects and women may be inessential, temporary and occasional. But it is felt as universal and malignant in Plath's work. The texture of her poetry, more than any view implied in it, is her refutation of that discourse.

9

SEAMUS HEANEY

I

Like Ted Hughes, whom he admired and emulated, Heaney began with an aggressive urge to punish the pastoral and 'Romantic' expectations of his readers. *Death of a Naturalist* is the title of his first book.[1] It is ambiguous, and might properly refer to a zoologist or a Zolaist. In fact it is a malapropism for the death of one who feels Romantic idealism in the face of Nature. Whatever doubt there may be about the title, there is none about the poems: blackberries turn sour and mouldy ('Blackberry Picking'), kittens are drowned ('The Early Purges'). And it is not only idealized feeling for nature that is punished, but also the Romantic conception of the child's innocence. Many of the poems relate the disillusioning experiences of a child on an Ulster farm. Thus, at the end of 'Blackberry Picking' we have:

> I always felt like crying. It wasn't fair
> That all the lovely canfuls smelt of rot.
> Each year I hoped they'd keep, knew they would not.

Here even the child's voice intrudes. And in 'The Early Purges' the speaker says that he was 6 when he first saw kittens drown: 'Still, living displaces false sentiments.' The language of the poems is intended to be appropriate to this process in its Hughesian harshness and evasion of the mellifluous: there is a sour delight in 'the squelch and slap / Of soggy peat, the curt cuts of an edge / Through living roots' ('Digging'), even in the frogs that terrified him out of his innocent childish world of collecting tadpoles and frogspawn:

> Right down the dam gross-bellied frogs were cocked
> On sods; their loose necks pulsed like sails. Some hopped:
> The slap and plop were obscene threats. Some sat
> Poised like mud grenades, their blunt heads farting.
>
> ('Death of a Naturalist')

The profession of poet is intended, at this stage in his career, to impart to the reader the rude but salutary education afforded by life on the farm. This is one of the meanings of 'Digging', where the poet, writing, looks out to where his father is digging: 'Between my finger and my thumb / The squat pen rests. / I'll dig with it.'

Like Hughes, Heaney chooses a striking metaphorical style with which to bludgeon the reader into an acceptance of his tough vision. And as with Hughes, the impression conveyed is one of isolation and alienation. Indeed, 'Digging' takes for its subject Heaney's position as an insider become alienated: the college boy returning to the farm where he grew up. Both distant and intimate he looks down on his father through a window, separated by a pane of glass. From this point of view digging represents the recovery of the past, of intimate relationship. The style of 'foregrounding the metaphor', as I call it (taking a hint from Terence Hawkes), suggests intimacy in its vividness even as, in its artificiality and its need for startling transformation, it suggests alienation.[2] Indeed, the metaphorical style could be called 'the recovered intimacy of the alienated': a description reminiscent of Romantic philosophy. Heaney's work in general, at this stage, contains a thoroughly post-Romantic amalgam, characteristic of the twentieth century: on the one hand he chastises idealism and uses metaphors of machinery to depict the natural (in 'Trout' the fish hangs 'a fat gun-barrel' and 'darts like a tracer- / bullet'); on the other, he displays a tough nostalgia for his own origins and for their rootedness, which can only be described as Romantic, and which patently looks back, through Hardy and Edward Thomas, to Wordsworth.

The isolated ingenuity of each metaphor or simile makes some poems seem like displays of verbal fireworks: the effort at intimacy is strained, as in this from *Death of a Naturalist*:

> Clouds ran their wet mortar, plastered the daybreak
> Grey. The stones clicked tartly
> If we missed the sleepers but mostly
> Silent we headed up the railway
> Where now the only steam was funneling from cows
> Ditched on their rumps beyond hedges . . .
> The rails scored a bull's eye into the eye
> Of a bridge. A corncrake challenged
> Unexpectedly like a hoarse sentry.
>
>   ('Dawn Shoot')

And so on. As Andrew Crozier well says, discussing Heaney's poem 'The Barn',

> the tropes proliferate and are uniformly highlighted, like consumer goods in a shop window, but they are uncoordinated . . . the effect is gratuitous and draws attention finally to the poet's rhetorical ingenuity. Everything is of a piece, irrespective of what is being said. Our sense that the details bind together into a more complex meaning derives not from the figures but from the attenuated presence of autobiographical anecdote.[3]

The tendency towards this kind of writing has been accelerated by Craig Raine and other so-called Metaphor Men.

In discussing the considerable influence of Philip Hobsbaum on Heaney and other young poets at the Queen's University, Belfast, in the 1960s, Blake Morrison has this to say: 'it is clear that [Hobsbaum] favoured a poetry that combined the wit and metrical tightness of the Movement with the power and physicality of Ted Hughes, a combination his young Derry protege achieved only too well.'[4] The wit and the metrical tightness may be more in evidence than in Hughes, but neither quality is noteworthy for any other reason. And though he courts a discursive manner more than Hughes does, it is seldom with the development of argument the reader half expects: endings tend to be abandoned with a sudden epigram. So the poem is largely a recording of an incident in the past by means of small metaphorical transcriptions of the moments that compose it. The discursive manner, when it is there, derives from the need to frame the incident in the past.

As much as Hughes, Heaney gives the impression of insecurity and self-division in these poems. Yet like Hughes, and probably for the same reason, Heaney regards the tough pose he adopts as a 'masculine' type of assertiveness — at least, this is, as we shall see, a very reasonable deduction from these remarks of his on Hughes in the collection of essays, *Preoccupations*: 'His consonants are the Norsemen, the Roundheads in the world of his vocables, hacking and hedging and hammering down the abundance and luxury and possible lasciviousness of the vowels.'[15]

II

Heaney's exploration of origins has always been undertaken on behalf of his nation as well as himself. His own childhood was seen as a museum of experiences typical of a vanishing way of life, and his exhibits of traditional peasant farming ways have the effect of making him a representative figure. But the exploration was soon coaxed into a wider scope by the pressure to say something significant about the Northern Irish Troubles. To date his most extended and ambitious response to that pressure is still to be found in the so-called Bog Poems in *North*, a loose series instigated in large part by his reading of the archaeologist P. V. Glob's 1969 book, *The Bog People*.[6] This work records the discovery of the preserved bodies of Iron Age men and women in the bogs of Denmark. They appear to be ritual victims. Several connections with Ireland were apparent: the bog itself, which in both countries preserved prehistoric corpses and artifacts; the association in each with Viking culture (see Heaney's 'Viking Dublin' in *North*); and the possibility that the ancient religion of both countries was based on the worship of a mother goddess who demanded propitiation with human sacrifice, or ensured fertility as a result of it. This last point sets off a complex train of thought in Heaney's mind, which goes a long way towards explaining how he could think of the Troubles and of Iron Age Denmark in the same light. As he says:

You have a society in the Iron Age where there was ritual blood-letting.
You have a society where girls' heads were shaved for adultery, you have a
religion centring on the territory, on a goddess of the ground and of the
land, and associated with sacrifice. Now in many ways the fury of Irish
Republicanism is associated with a religion like this, with a female
goddess who appeared in various guises. She appears as Cathleen ni
Houlihan in Yeats's plays; she appears as Mother Ireland. I think that the
Republican ethos is a feminine religion, in a way. It seems to me that
there are satisfactory imaginative parallels between this religion and time
and our own time.[7]

And so, with a sense of exploring an undisciplined and emotional
culture of blood, soil and vengeance, which he regards as feminine,
Heaney starts a deeper digging into the bog of history. The poems
themselves are short-lined, and look long and vertical on the page. In
this they have been influenced in part by short-lined medieval Gaelic
lyrics, so that they represent a deeper pursuit of poetic origins at the
same time that, visually, they represent a vertical sinking into the layers
of the bog.

The Bog Poems provide yet another example of the isolated poetic
observer seeking to invest the chaos of history with some general meaning. Like the Romantic poets, and like all post-Romantic poets who
have attempted it, Heaney is putting together a mythology of his own.
And like many, particularly in the modern period, he is doing it, so to
speak, from spare parts lying around. As often happens, he uses these
parts in such an idiosyncratic way that the large general gesture serves
only to emphasize still further the isolation of the poet. One may put
these poems alongside Hughes's *Crow* or Thom Gunn's *Misanthropos*, or
especially Hill's *Mercian Hymns* and David Jones's *Anathemata*, to both of
which they are indebted. Or one may place them at the end of a line of
descent from Blake and Shelley through Pound and Eliot.

An instructive poem with which to illustrate this condition of
Heaney's poems, as well as their particular characteristics, is 'Punishment', in *North*. Here the speaker considers the body of an Iron Age
woman preserved by the bog into which she was cast, probably as the
penalty for adultery:

> I can feel the tug
> of the halter at the nape

of her neck, the wind
on her naked front.

It blows her nipples
to amber beads,
it shakes the frail rigging
of her ribs.

Why is it important to mention the imagining of her nipples and ribs?
It verges on the gratuitous, or it would do if the poem were simply a
description of a shrivelled, preserved corpse. But of course it is not: it is
very overtly the observer's interpretation. Hence the emphasis on the
speaker ('I can feel . . .'; 'I can see her drowned / body in the bog . . .').
Heaney is self-aware enough to have included himself (or the speaker).
He compares the punishment of the Iron Age girl with that of young
Northern Irish Catholic women, tarred and feathered for going out with
squaddies. It is a rich passage, suggesting simple fear; the infirm,
compromised neutrality of the liberal; the guilt of the male sex for acts
of patriarchal cruelty towards women; and even a troubled sense, also
present in the mildly sadistic lines quoted above, that male sexuality is
always tending towards such cruelty:

I almost love you
but would have cast, I know,
the stones of silence.
I am the artful voyeur

of your brain's exposed
and darkened combs,
your muscles' webbing
and all your numbered bones;

I who have stood dumb
when your betraying sisters,
cauled in tar,
wept by the railings,

who would connive
in civilized outrage
yet understand the exact
and tribal, intimate revenge.

This observer, detached from, yet intimate with, his tribe, is indisting-
uishable in his social stance from the young man who figures in *Death of
a Naturalist*. What that young man does with his array of ingenious
little metaphors is much the same as what the poet of *North* does with
his grand inclusive one: it is to make a gesture at giving meaning to a
fragmentary and inexplicable world in such a way that the world remains
essentially fragmentary and inexplicable. A condition of this process is
that the metaphors seem subjective: desperate, if energetic, throws of
the isolated consciousness. In historical terms the comparison of Northern Ireland with Iron Age Europe, as an explanation of the Troubles, can
scarcely be rivalled in absurdity. The very details in which the comparison is conveyed (the similarity of tar to the black sheen of the preserved
corpse) almost invite one to recognize their speciousness from a purely
explanatory point of view: they insist on the subjective nature of the
connection.

Yet this is not to impugn Heaney. The sophistication with which he
insists that his vision is indeed personal, even as he questions his own
position, makes it clear that these poems should not be considered under
the category of historical explanations, failed or not. They represent the
self-examination of the troubled, isolated modern consciousness. In any
case, what would a scientifically historical poem about Northern Ireland
be like, if such a thing can be imagined? Different from Heaney,
perhaps, but hardly free of metaphor, which I take to be a condition of
most interpretation, against those neo-objectivists who recommend its
elimination from writing.

But to return to Heaney's vision. I used the word 'patriarchal' to
describe similar acts of cruelty towards women. And this act does take a
form reminiscent of vengeance against women in some strongly patriarchal societies ('cast . . . / the stones'). Nor can Heaney seriously believe
that modern Ireland is in any profound sense dominated by women,
whatever he believes of Iron Age Denmark. Yet, by his own account, he
sees Irish Republicanism as representing a 'feminine' religion. It would
seem that this religion, for Heaney, is as much to do with an irrational
mode of consciousness as with anything supported by institutions and
definite social practice. Certainly he is a strong believer in the words
'masculine' and 'feminine' as denoting two modes of consciousness, and
two corresponding kinds of poetic practice. This is made very clear in
his Chatterton lecture on Hopkins (1974):

In the masculine mode, the language functions as a form of address, of assertion and command, and the poetic effort has to do with conscious quelling and control of the materials, a labour of shaping; words are not music before they are anything else, nor are they drowsy from their slumber in the unconscious, but athletic, capable, displaying the muscle of sense. Whereas in the feminine mode the language functions more as evocation than as address, and the poetic effort is not so much a labour of design as it is an act of divination and revelation; words in the feminine mode behave with the lover's come hither instead of the athlete's display, they constitute a poetry that is delicious as texture before it is recognised as architectonic.[8]

Where the manner of *Death of a Naturalist*, with its hacking consonants, had been preponderantly 'masculine', that of the Bog Poems is supposed to be 'feminine'. There may be less substantial difference than Heaney implies, since he has never been a strongly argumentative poet. But there is a relative looseness and freedom about these later poems, a relative lack of intrusive figures and alliterative bluntness, and also a languorous caressing of fine words, which correspond to his description.

But there is something ambiguous about this 'femininity'. Here this is a quality associated with both ancient Celtic and Norse culture. Yet he had earlier attributed hacking consonants to 'Norsemen', as we saw above. And that was in a context where Norsemen connoted control over lascivious vowels, a control which we have to see as part of his 'masculine' mode. In 'Traditions' (*Wintering Out*)[9] he refers to the way in which the Irish 'guttural muse / was bulled long ago / by the alliterative tradition', a statement which makes Gaelic the passive feminine, deflowered by the rough masculine Teuton – an enactment of the larger rape committed on Ireland by England: 'Ralegh has backed the maid to a tree / As Ireland is backed to England' ('Ocean's Love to Ireland', *North*). Heaney's savage, feminine, northern religion dissolves the boundaries between the opposites it comprises: Celt and Teuton, Catholic and Protestant, male and female. Heaney's feminine religion is his own divided post-colonial consciousness, in which he himself may identify with both dominant and subordinate – linguistically and culturally. But there seems to be no way beyond these mutually neutralizing opposites within their own terms. It is as if little could be said that would not contribute to that savage system. Heaney's recent solution is to try and stand outside it, to discover a demythologized way to talk about Ireland, and things other than Ireland, in a state of wakeful and unobsessed isolation. *Sweeney Astray*, his translation of the mediaeval saga *Buile Shuibhne* ('The Frenzy of Sweeeney') certainly suggests a liberation from the 'tribal, intimate' norms and assumptions of Ireland.[10] Its hero, Sweeney, a king from County Antrim, Ulster, insults St Ronan, and is driven into a life of wandering. It is interesting to note that Heaney suppresses the idea of 'frenzy' in the title. And in his introduction he refers to 'the quarrel between free creative imagination and the constraints of religious, political and domestic obligation'. This need for untrammelled artistic expression finds a memorable voice in the sequence of poems called 'Station Island' (from the volume with the same title).[11] The series concerns a pilgrimage to the island of Patrick's Purgatory in Lough Derg, County Donegal (Ulster, but in the Republic). Pilgrims there perform penances, each part of which is called a 'station'. The final poem, in liberal *terza rima*, has Joyce appearing like Brunetto Latini, counselling Heaney in this wise:

> That subject people stuff is a cod's game,
> infantile, like your peasant pilgrimage . . .
> . . .
>
> When they make the circle wide, it's time to swim
>
> out on your own and fill the element
> with signatures on your own frequency . . .

Scattered through the volume are some intimations of anxiety about pursuing this course. In 'Away from it All', a lobster fished from its tank for the leisurely consumption of the speaker is contrasted with those that have remained behind:

> And I still cannot clear my head
> of lives in their element
> on the cobbled floor of that tank
> and the hampered one, out of water,
> fortified and bewildered.

The convivial eating attributed to the speaker makes being away from it all seem benign, health-giving, 'fortifying' in the best sense. But his

figurative kinship with the lobster is ominous: is he out of his social
element? Is worse to follow? And what is it to be in one's element?
While he ate, a few lines from Czeslaw Milosz had occurred to him:

> *I was stretched between contemplation*
> *of a motionless point*
> *and the command to participate*
> *actively in history.*

His companion asks: '*Actively?* What do you mean?' The line about 'lives
in their element' indicate that Heaney is not sure. Does one participate
in history 'actively' in a consciously political sense, or does one do this
by a semi-conscious immersion in the element of one's tribe? It seems
clear that Heaney has opted for neither course. The freedom he seeks is
more neutral than that, a matter of 'echo soundings, searches, probes'
as he expresses it through the mouth of Joyce at the end of 'Station
Island'. And this means, among other things, saying goodbye to the
Goddess and the feminine religion. He does so, gently but firmly, and
almost by her own admonition, in 'Sheelagh na Gig', also from *Station
Island*. A Sheelagh na Gig is an obscene female figure sculpted on early
medieval churches in Ireland (from whence it is thought to originate),
western France and central England. This particular one is at Kilpeck
church in Herefordshire, and was the subject of a collection of poems,
including Heaney's, by various hands, *The Kilpeck Anthology*.[12] It is not
unreasonable to suppose that the figure reflects a Celtic goddess cult, and
presumably Heaney was aware of this possibility. At the end of the
poem he describes her as,

> grown-up, grown ordinary,
> seeming to say,
> 'Yes, look at me to your heart's content
>
> but look at every other thing.'
> And here is a leaper in a kilt,
> two figures kissing,
>
> a mouth with sprigs,
> a running hart, two fishes,
> a damaged beast with an instrument.

She is sanctioning Heaney's relatively dispassionate stance, allowing him to think about the feminine religion of Ireland, or to delight in life and nature, in a context removed from the myths and nightmares of his country, as he pleases. Perhaps it is easier for him to do this when all that turmoil has been displaced onto the Other of the feminine.

10

CRAIG RAINE

I

The tendency towards a kind of writing that makes a display of its ingenuity in finding metaphors or similes for things seen has been accelerated by Craig Raine and other so-called Metaphor Men. But in the case of Raine it is not usually 'autobiographical anecdote' that occasionally strives to unite the desultory figures: it is the fact of alienation itself:

> We live in the great indoors:
> the vacuum cleaner grazes
> over the carpet, lowing,
> its udder a swollen wobble . . .
>
> At night the switches stare
> from every wall like flat-faced
> barn-owls, and light ripens
> the electric pear.
> ('An Enquiry into Two Inches of Ivory'.)[1]

Here the visualization of domestic objects in pastoral terms ironically underscores the alienated separation from nature, as well as presenting that alienation by distancing and making strange the familiar objects of house-bound, isolated modern life.

There is a parallel to this metaphorical poetry of domestic alienation in the work of Sylvia Plath. In the case of Plath, alienation is the schizophrenic's detached anxiety, as when she gazes dispassionately at her cut thumb in the kitchen ('Cut', quoted above in chapter 8), or in another kitchen scene in 'Lesbos':

> The potatoes hiss.
> It is all Hollywood, windowless,
> The fluorescent light wincing on and off like a terrible migraine.

Plath's metaphors have a high degree of consistency with each other, as we have seen: they will be grouped into several overlapping categories representing separate ideas, about which the poem is a kind of discussion.

For Raine, on the other hand, detachment is a mode of observation. Plath fills the world with meaning derived from emotional disturbance; Raine, on the other hand, empties it of all but, occasionally, a consistency of mood, or what adds up to a fairly uncontroversial statement about, say, children. Plath's is a rich expressionist poetry; Raine's is grounded in the notion of the objective as translated by a cool, ingenious observer. In 'An Enquiry into Two Inches of Ivory' the first two stanzas, quoted above, might lead one to expect a pertinacious exploitation of the indoor-pastoral idea. But no: that metaphor is dropped and is followed by others which serve merely to describe the object with witty precision:

> Daily things. Objects
> in the museum of ordinary art.
> Two armless Lilliputian queens
> preside, watching a giant bathe.
> He catches the slippery cubist fish
> with perfumed eggs. Another
> is a yogi on the scrubbing brush.
> Water painlessly breaks his bent
> Picasso legs.

The emphasis on 'Daily things' can be seen as an attempt to link Raine's practice with the Romantic ambition to present ordinary things in an unusual way. Yet there is no whiff of transcendence here, and Raine's post-Romantic inheritance comes from the aesthetic line beginning in Keats, rather than from that of Wordsworth. The rediscovery of familiar things is identified with 'art', and hence Raine's practice of using comparison for rediscovery is also identified with art. This fact supports David Trotter's claim that, 'The skill defined and over-defined by the work of Raine and Reid is the skill which has become in our society a sign for the entire scope and value of poetry.'[2] Whatever society's expectations (and there is much truth in what Trotter claims about this) Raine himself does identify comparison with the entire scope and value of poetry. And it does not matter whether or not the comparisons add up to any larger statement about the world Raine inhabits than simply that it is pleasing to see things clearly. One may be tempted, as in the case of the pastoral imagery, to see the references to Cubism as implying something about an unexpected analytic view of the object. But these are only two references out of many. They have to consort also with Lilliputian queens and a yogi on the scrubbing brush. The collocation leaves one feeling that the references to Cubism are on all fours with the other metaphors, and are merely there to provide more striking comparisons.

And how true is it really that one is seeing things anew? In fact, because the metaphors tend to come from widely disparate and sometimes exotic sources, because they tend to remain separate from each other, the reader catches at the visual likeness in the comparison and registers the familiar object very clearly, but does not feel that objects have been transformed or seen afresh. As far as seeing the object is concerned, this is all there is: what Raine calls 'seeing things very clearly', not seeing things anew.[3] So the blurb's claim, in *The Onion, Memory*, that 'Daily things . . . are shown to possess an extraordinary and often neglected poetry' must be qualified. Daily things are seen very clearly. The extraordinary poetry runs alongside them in a parallel but separate path, contributing a toll of visual similitude. But the exotic or humorous element in the comparison remains detached from the object, gesturing towards the poet's ingenuity and well-stocked mind. Thus, when we are told that 'Cups commemorate the War / of Jenkins' Ear', the comparison almost effaces itself in its own erudite incongruity. And though this does not always happen with a Raine metaphor, it is a common malady.

II

The reference to Lilliput can serve as a reminder that Raine imitates the Swiftian and Enlightenment ruse of introducing a foreign traveller to the everyday world. Swift's way of making Europe seem strange is to tamper with the perspective on things and people, reducing them or inflating them. But it is not so different a strategy from that of introducing a Chinese traveller to England, as Goldsmith does in *A Citizen of the World*. In *A Martian Sends a Postcard Home*, Raine introduces an alien to our planet.[4] Not surprisingly he finds people as strange as objects. And in fact much of Raine's production is taken up with the strangeness of humans. The first poems in *The Onion, Memory*, for example, are about traders and shopkeepers, one poem each. One is reminded of 'the butcher, the baker, the candle-stick maker', and indeed Raine does wish to subvert such conventional and inattentive acceptance of these special-ists. There is little to say about these entertaining sketches, except, perhaps, to take note of their characteristic gesturing at something more than the entertaining. 'The Grocer', for instance, is provided with a noteworthy epigraph from Joyce: 'the Kingdom of God cometh not with observation.' This is not an aphorism from which Raine has learnt much. But it seems that he would like to. For this reason the poem, having engaged in a virtuoso description of the grocer's actions, ends like this:

> Coins are raked with trident hand,
> trickled into the till – palm out,
>
> with thumb crooked over the stigma,
> he smiles like a modest quattrocento Christ.

From one aspect this is plainly ironic: faintly reminiscent of Yeats's Paudeen, 'fumbling in a greasy till', the grocer can be compared with Christ at the visual level but seems in every other way antithetical to him. But this realization of unlikeness in likeness is given the status of an epiphany: by its placing of the grocer's values, by its position at the end of the poem, by its sacred overtones, and by the way the epigraph nudges us into endowing it with a significance beyond appearances. Yet that significance is in itself trite (grocers are materialists), far triter than the visual component of the comparison, which is strikingly vivid.

Another attempt at added significance is characteristic of Raine: the attempt to link the metaphors by drawing them from the same source (the pastoral metaphors in 'An Enquiry') thus imparting a consistence of view to the poet's eye. 'The Butcher' is introduced: 'Surrounded by sausages, the butcher stands / smoking a pencil like Isambard Kingdom Brunel.' Much description devoid of reference to Victorian engineers ends in these lines: 'At 10, he drinks his tea with the spoon held back, / and the *Great Eastern* goes straight to the bottom.' If the point of this were merely that the butcher is a kind of engineer, little would have been gained, indeed. But the connotations of the Victorian hero-as-engineer play their part in pointing to a masterly independence shared by the small tradesmen; and even in suggesting that such independence is increasingly outmoded. Yet the perception, though valid, is very much dependent on the poet's disposition to see the butcher in these terms. We have to take his word for it that the butcher looks 'like' Brunel, rather than that he merely finds it illuminating to think so. As for the cup being like *The Great Eastern*, this smacks of effort. As with the pastoral metaphors in 'An Enquiry', Raine's attempts here at image-linking are ineffectual. And in this case they seem arbitrary.

But perhaps the most significant fact about the group of poems on traders is its title: 'Yellow Pages'. This indicates the modern relationship between customer and trader: distanced by the telephone. Taken with several Victorian references in the poems it also suggests pages yellow with age. We thus have a double pointer to modern alienation: distant both in time and space from a vanishing world of vivid, independent crafts and trades.

III

It is difficult to imagine that Raine would be deeply unhappy at the accusation that he fails to impart much significance to his poems beyond seeing very clearly and a sense of alienation. As he says:

One of Joyce's pupils in Trieste recalled that Joyce used to make his students go away and describe, say, an oil lamp: the student coined the phrase 'descriptive lust' to evoke Joyce's aim. That's what I'm interested in ... I'm not interested in writing poems which end with thumping statements; I'm interested in making objects. I think poems are machines in the sense that Baudelaire called Delacroix's paintings machines; they have to work as artistic objects.[5]

The title of one of the sections of *The Onion, Memory* neatly conveys part of the attitude accompanying this ideal: 'The Significance of Nothing', ambivalently suggesting both the discovery of significance where none had discerned it before, and the nothingness of that significance. These are tales 'told by an idiot', and this, too, is an ambivalent fact: Raine, in his own estimation, is both the idiot as Romantic visionary and the idiot who knows nothing. But titles and texts frequently signal to the reader that it is pompous and boring to complain that there is nothing much going on in these poems: 'Wake up, see things clearly, if you're still child enough to be able to do so.'

But Raine persists, and becomes more ambitious, in his attempts to encompass the human world in the frail, gaudy vessels of his poems. The title poem of *A Martian Sends a Postcard Home* is not untypical in the way it alludes, very briefly, to the complexities of human life:

> Only the young are allowed to suffer
> openly. Adults go to a punishment room
>
> with water but nothing to eat.
> They lock the door and suffer the noises
>
> alone. No one is exempt
> and everyone's pain has a different smell.

In context, the statement about the open suffering of the young is arresting, coming as it does after a tricksy description of the use of telephones. When we are next told that 'Adults go to a punishment room ...', etc., we have been led to expect some reflection on suffering, and suspect that this will provide one about that of adults. When we discover that the Martian is describing lavatories, the joke is on him. He knows nothing about the real conditions of adult suffering. But the joke is also on us, who expected something of significance or pathos.

And it may be well that Raine should be cautious in the display of these qualities. Certainly they can lead him disastrously awry. The poem from *A Martian* about a Nazi officer, 'Oberfeldwebel Beckstadt', is an egregious example, in every way reminiscent of a bad, sentimental, morally dubious TV drama. The beginning sets the slipshod tone: 'It is the end of the war / and Oberfeldwebel Beckstadt / hasn't had time to shave.' You know how it is at the end of a war! But it is the end of the poem which is truly shocking:

> It is time to go home
> to a wife in curlers
>
> like a barrister,
> who will ask him questions,
>
> call him Otto
> and make him cry.

The characteristically arbitrary intrusion of the curlers–barrister simile (despite its connotations of innocence as judge) rings with an uncertain note, like a silly joke in a solemn context. The suggestion that the war may have been a nightmare for the officer we might just have been prepared to take, if the somewhat hackneyed pathos of the ending did not seem so placed as to solicit most of our sympathy for poor old Otto.

IV

Until the publication of *Rich*,[6] then, Raine might have seemed like an entertaining minor poet, capable of errors of judgement when he strayed outside his narrow scope. But there are unexpectedly accomplished things in *Rich*, and this advance can be attributed to several related changes of style. First, there is a salutary tendency towards the inclusion of the first-person narrator and observer. This admission of subjectivity has the effect of making the intense peculiarity of the poems seem less arbitrary. And then there is a considerable reduction in the number of astounding metaphors. And Raine manages his rhythm so that there is more sense of flow through the poem. This sense of continuity is aided by a more extensive deployment of the variety of syntax: the poem is no longer reduced to a staccato series of propositions. All aids consistency of view; and, fittingly, there are several successful essays in the linking of images.

A charming example of the new style can be found in 'In Modern Dress', a poem which revolves around the conceit that the speaker's child is like some Tudor discoverer, not only to look at, but also by virtue of the fact that he is an explorer of new worlds:

> Sir Walter Raleigh
> trails his comforter
> about the muddy garden,
>
> a full-length Hilliard
> in miniature hose
> and padded pants.
>
> How rakishly upturned
> his fine moustache
> of oxtail soup,
>
> foreshadowing, perhaps,
> some future time
> of altered favour,
>
> stuck in the high chair
> like a pillory, features
> pelted with food.

Raine watches his child pondering 'the potato / in its natural state / for the very first time', and ends by considering his own relationship with the child as that of courtier to kind. But there are other examples of the new style which are better than charming. 'A Walk in the Country', for instance, which begins with the speaker and his daughter walking out 'beyond the sewage farm'. This is memorably described as

> like a tape-recorder,
> whose black spools
> turn night and day
>
> as excrement
> patiently eavesdrops
> on peace.

It is a machine
that remembers
the sounds of nothing . . .

The sewage farm becomes a metaphor for a limit to ordinary experience
at which point the travellers enter a realm where the nothingness of
death must be faced: a graveyard surrounded by the fire of stubble-
burning, flames which seem infernal, if only because of the poem's
epigraph from Dante. This is a place of fear. But,

One swallow
sways on a wire
like a grain

of whiskered barley
saved from the flames.

And this is not merely a fine visual simile, but also a metaphor for the
triumph of life over death, a metaphor which gathers strength from the
Biblical conception of the seed dying and being reborn. The church is
being re-roofed. And in the graveyard is a man

gardening a grave

methodically,
lost in the rituals
of growth.

Growth from the excremental results of death, that is. And then the
speaker rolls away a stone with his foot, to find

this toad
with acorn eyes

and a brown body
delicate as a drop
of dusty water

yet still intact
and hardly surprised
by resurrection.

The small brown body amidst the dirt combines both the ideas of excrement and those of growth: again, life out of death. This is also a resurrection from hell, for the element of water has triumphed over its opposite, fire. The image confirms that the two walkers have survived, with optimism, their glimpse of the nothingness of death. And retrospectively it confirms the warmth of the speaker's tenderness for the new life in his daughter's veins, and underlines his implicit reassurance to her that the vision of death is not one that should overwhelm hope and energy. As he says to her earlier on, 'Do not be afraid.'

V

It is not entirely surprising to find Raine exercising his talent for the recording of sensation where the effect will be most titillating: on sex. In the *Martian* volume there had been the poem 'Sexual Couplets', which had simply transferred the Raine technique of familiar-made-strangely-familiar to a moment of sexual intercourse:

> My shoe-tree wants to come
> and stretch your body where it lies undone . . .
>
> I am wearing a shiny souwester;
> you are coxcombed like a jester . . .
>
> Oh my strangely gutted one,
> the fish head needs your flesh around its bone . . .

Considered as a visual recording this is not markedly inferior or superior to most of Raine's other efforts. But the fact that sex is the subject may excite an ambivalent feeling in the reader. The visual exactness is mildly titillatory, but the whimsical effect of the metaphors imparts an air of the comic to the whole proceedings: looked at from one point of view, one can see the justice in this: sex is funny. From another point of view, though, it seems as if Raine is inviting a prurient snigger. For the 'sex is funny' perspective would seem to belong more appropriately to the satirist, standing outside the action. But the speaker in Raine's poem is one of those involved, and seems to be inviting us to share both the excitement and the sense of the comic, so that 'sniggering' does seem a more appropriate word for the total effect.

A similar effect is achieved by different means in the poem 'Gauguin', from *Rich*, of which these lines are an example:

> He stickyout number 2 tongue
> because he magnetized to she.

> Which she hide in shesecrets
> because she magnetized to he.
> They making the mirror, shhh,
> numberonetongues completely tied.

> Shebody making the horse
> and the frog, the safe shescissor,

> the squat on sheback, showing
> shekipper tenminute longtime . . .

Here the prurient snigger lies in the nature of the translation set for the reader: from the amusingly inept English and apt images, to an extremely blatant picture of *coitus a tergo*. There are a number of other poems about sex in *Rich*, and all of them convey the same sense of titillatory objectification – a fitting adjunct to Raine's frequently sensationalist practice in other areas.

It is appropriate that, in 'Gauguin', we should be offered the translation of an event into pidgin English. For this is a reasonable extension into the linguistic sphere of the attitude of the innocent but alienated observer. This is not the first time that Raine has married linguistic to perceptual dislocation. The first poem in 'Anno Domini', from *The Onion, Memory*, is 'The Corporation Gardener's Prologue' which gives us the gardener's view of John, the faith-healer hero of the sequence.

> Deedoadal John on Sadder daies, on margged daies, in cass-doff ladies'
> camel coad, in sangwedge board – an aygell wooded-wigged – falsetter
> voyse, cryigg: rebend, rebend, for evans add and.

The gestures towards the polyvalency of *Finnegans Wake* ('Wooded-wigged', 'rebend') are too occasional and too trivial to count for much, and the total effect is of a puerile rendering of an adenoidal voice.

There is a faint echo of the Adam-language here. But there is also a hint that Raine is at least slightly self-conscious not just about his metaphorical method but also about the implied position of the observer in his poems. This first seems to be confirmed in a playful poem from *Rich* called 'A Free Translation' where everything is seen in the light of oriental associations: a 'pagoda / of dirty dinner plates', a skein of wool that is 'a geisha girl with skewered hair' and so on. There is no reason for the translation except a whim and the pleasure it brings. But, by giving this factitious consistency to his imagery Raine is in effect admitting that his method is not just a 'seeing clearly' but also a translation into the terms set by an alienated observer.

It would be foolish to be too dismissive of Raine. His poems offer pleasure, of a narrow kind, that it is pointless to try and exclude from poetry. And the appeal of such pleasure is not based merely on the witty ingenuity which is so large a part of its cause, but also a feeling of kinship between reader and poet inhabiting equally a society marked by alienation. It is not because Raine offers us either a strange or a familiar world that he is popular, but because we all recognize how strange the familiar can be. But if Raine is to be anything more than an accomplished minor poet, he will have to question and place the role of the observer in his poems: why does this now seem like a good way of seeing things? Some of the poems in *Rich* give grounds for hope that Raine would be capable of developing in this way. His adaptations of Pasternak (*The Electrification of the Soviet Union* (1986)) and of Racine ('*1953*' (1990)) reinforce this hope, though it is interesting to note that they pay respects to two Modernist idols: the mechanical and the neo-Classical.

POSTMODERNISM: THE RETURN OF
THE SUPPRESSED

Perhaps the surest sign that the poetry of things is on the way out in the
United States is the celebrity of John Ashbery. Neither the celebrity nor
even the name have fared so well in Britain, where occasionally reviewers
such as Tom Paulin or John Carey will devote a few loftily contemp-
tuous words to what they deem to be the obvious badness of the strange
poetry produced by this mysterious admirer of modern painting and
French literature. Badness when compared with the poetry of things,
that is. The taste of what has so provoked some critics may be sampled
from the following lines at the beginning of a longish poem from *The
Tennis Court Oath*:[1]

> How much longer will I be able to inhabit the divine sepulcher
> Of life, my great love? Do dolphins plunge bottomward
> To find the light? Or is it rock
> That is searched? Unrelentingly? Huh. And if some day
>
> Men with orange shovels come to break open the rock
> Which encases me, what about the light that comes in then?
> What about the smell of the light?
> What about the moss?
>
> In pilgrim times he wounded me
> Since then I only lie
> My bed of light is a furnace choking me
> With hell (and sometimes I hear salt water dripping).

I mean it – because I'm one of the few
To have held my breath under the house. I'll trade
One red sucker for two blue ones. I'm
Named Tom.
('How Much Longer Will I Be Able to Inhabit the Divine Sepulcher')

A flagrant parody of the high Romantic manner, none too irreverent for modern tastes, is followed by discordant registers ('Huh'; 'I'll trade / One red sucker for two blue ones'), topics ('Men with orange shovels'), fragments of narrative ('In pilgrim times he wounded me / Since then I only lie') and implied speakers ('I mean it because I'm one of the few / To have held my breath under the house'). The effect is not unlike that of Breton's surrealism, in its Romantic manner and sense of dream logic (things are definitely happening *underneath*) except that there is a more playful interest in the clash of registers here: more indebtedness to the collage principle, then. This garrulous poem teases us into interpretation: it offers us a fanfare of a beginning; a fine cadence of an ending, as it happens; something that almost adds up to a narrative; and something that almost adds up to image-linking. It is, then, the parody of a poem, though one which conveys considerable care and artifice in the making. An analogy with abstract expressionism suggests itself, in that the poem seems to be far less interested in reference than in the patterns that can be taken by its medium.

Such effects are characteristic of any of Ashbery's volumes, although there has been a gradual increase in coherence and continuity. But another technique is to work with larger blocks of what looks like continuous material, only to explode the reader's expectations yet again with a different kind of block, as in these lines from *Self-Portrait in a Convex Mirror*:[2]

'Once I let a guy blow me.
I kind of backed away from the experience.
Now years later, I think of it
Without emotion . . .'
                                        ('Poem in Three Parts")

But then a few lines later:

> The day fries with a fine conscience,
> Shadows, ripples, underbrush, old cars.
> The conscience is to you as what is known,
> The unknowable gets to be known.

The camp, dead-pan parody, which he shares with Frank O'Hara and
Kenneth Koch, is weighted by passages quite unlike the characteristic
work of the New York School: hair-splitting meditations reminiscent of
Stevens at his driest, or surreal scenes which clearly owe something to
early Auden ('In a far recess of summer / Monks are playing soccer' –
lines from the early volume *Some Trees*).[3] But about much of Ashbery's
work there is a fascinating panache of diction and phrasing which sends
the reader back to the poems repeatedly, wondering, can this be
meaningless? How do we domesticate this wild pet?

Ashbery throws out a challenge to present readers' assumptions as
great as that once offered by Eliot or Pound. But is it even a challenge of
the same kind as theirs? Unlikely. A traditional account of the reading
of Modernist poems is that we reconstruct, from artfully juxtaposed
fragments, the meaning, which forms as a sediment between the gaps in
the text and the fragmentary text itself: we may be reconstructing
different kinds of history in Lowell and Pound, and different criteria
may be used to do so, but there is a broad similarity of technique.

Jonathan Culler has tried this method on Ashbery's 'They Dream
Only of America'.[4] The attempt is illuminating, for it brings out certain
areas of reference – the American Dream, the detective story (this last
used as a symbol for the reader's attempts at sense-making). It must be
said that Culler offers his conclusions tentatively, as an example of
possible naturalizations of this text. But the general air of coherence is
unconvincing. It seems likely that the attempt to find coherent meaning
in much of Ashbery, especially the early work, is sufficiently close to
reductionism to be misleading. The contrast with classic Modernism is
helpful, however, because it clarifies the fact that most of his poems
(there are exceptions) do not gesture beyond themselves: any inferences
we make must be from the method of the poems as a whole, and not
from individual parts of them. Ashbery seeks to elicit our delight first of
all in his medium itself, and secondly in its fitness to act as a poetic
version of the stream of consciousness: we are not enjoined to look
beyond such words as this:

> I tried each thing, only some were immortal and free.
> Elsewhere we are as sitting in a place where sunlight
> Filters down, a little at a time,
> Waiting for someone to come. Harsh words are spoken,
> As the sun yellows the green of the maple tree . . .
> ('As One Put Drunk onto the Packet-Boat')

To be artless about his meaning, but artful in representing it, is one of the chief things that Ashbery has attempted. Except that he has reasons for doing so. And, as reasons will, these crop up, not so artlessly, in the poems.

Some critics attempt to see him as looking at 'reality' in an unusual way. This is probably helpful if one does not take it too seriously – in which case it becomes positively misleading. Reality for Ashbery is only apprehended through language and convention, especially literary convention. As with Joyce's *Ulysses*, one may occasionally think in terms of an extreme naturalism, only to be forcibly confronted with a highly circumspect and ironic awareness of the role played by convention in producing the effect of reality.

Ashbery constructs a floridly rhetorical and sententious poetic language, capable of encompassing the banal and the irrelevant, in which to render the meanderings of the mind – clearly a mind bewilderingly sensitive to the odd and the contingent, and all that evades a neat, inclusive interpretation. And interpretation itself becomes one of the main themes, set amid all the grand inconsequence. Interpretation is the subsumption of a million lovely details under some grey illusory essence:

> Is anything central?
> Orchards flung out on the land,
> Urban forests, rustic plantations, knee-high hills?
> Are place names central?
> ('The One Thing That Can Save America', *Self-Portrait*)

The answer is no: 'These are connected to my version of America / But the juice is elsewhere.' And in general Ashbery seems to think that the only knowledge worth having is of minute particulars:

> Too bad I mean that getting to know each just for a fleeting second
> Must be replaced by imperfect knowledge of the featureless whole

Like some pocket history of the world, so general
As to constitute a sob or wail unrelated
To any attempt at definition.

('Grand Galop', *Self-Portrait*)

To know the sum of things would be to transcend – or fall beneath –
language. What really interests Ashbery, he pretends, is detail, flux, the
'weather': "What precisely is it / About the time of day it is, the
weather, that casuses people to note it painstakingly in their diaries
. . .?" ('Grand Galop'). We are constrained to details in any case by the
nature of language: partial words do not permit access to any whole:
'changes are merely / Features of the whole'. And, 'there are no words for
the surface, that is / No words to say what it really is, that it is not /
Superficial but a visible core' ('Self-Portrait in a Convex Mirror').

These reflections are the rationale for the digressive and inconsequen-
tial movement of the poems, and for the farcical parody that enlivens
them. For literary conventions are a device, Ashbery implies, for interpreting the world in accordance with some tired, respectable, as Barthes
would say 'readable', notion of reality, which pretends that it is the
natural point of view, whereas it has a transient and determinate history.
Literary conventions make things easier on reader and writer by ex-
tracting essences. In 'Forties Flick', from *Self-Portrait*, Ashbery meditates
on the ending of a film:

Why must it always end this way?
A dais with woman reading, with the ruckus of her hair
And all that is unsaid about her pulling us back to her, with her
Into the silence that night alone can't explain.
Silence of the library, of the telephone with its pad,
But we didn't have to reinvent these either:
They had gone away into the plot of a story,
The 'art' part – knowing what important details to leave out
And the way character is developed. Things too real
To be of much concern, hence artificial, yet now all over the page
The indoors with the outside becoming part of you
As you find you had never left off laughing at death,
The background, dark vine at the edge of the porch.

The last lines suggest that the background, the frame and the important details left out of the plot are symbols of death: they cannot be assimilated to those constructions of ourselves and the world which we imagine to be the sum of our life. That we are inserted into what we miscall a background is a fact that bears the threat of annihilation to the insecure ego. I suspect that Ashbery, with his knowledge of contemporary French thought, may owe something to the influence of Lacan here, who, in his seminar on 'Anamorphosis', uses Holbein's 'Ambassadors', with its hidden, distorted skull, as a comparable emblem of the conflict between the Imaginary and the Symbolic.[5]

The assault on conventional interpretations can be fairly aggressive, encompassing vicious and hilarious parodies of the mythologies, emblems and stereotypes of contemporary society. Thus, in 'Daffy Duck in Hollywood' (in *Houseboat Days*),[6] we are treated to the spectacle of that character as a kind of fallen Satan in the Hell of contemporary Hollywood, where every cultural fact is on a level with any other, and all are judged according to some facile notion of style: whenever Daffy hears La Celestina sing he is reminded, of all things, of:

> a mint-condition can
> Of Rumford's Baking Powder, a celluloid earring, Speedy
> Gonzales, the latest from Helen Topping Miller's fertile
> Escritorie, a sheaf of suggestive pix on greige, deckle-edged
> Stock.

Anything can have style in the array of artifacts, even art. Even Nature, as long as that too can be referred to something in the array:

> Just now a magnetic storm hung in the swatch of sky
> Over the Fudds' garage, reducing it – drastically –
> To the aura of a plumbago-blue log cabin on
> A Gadsden Purchase commemorative cover.

Much is implied in that one word 'drastically'. For Daffy, like Satan, is unhappy in his fallenness, aware of his loss. Among the voices he is given is the Miltonic, in which he has this to say: 'while I / Abroad through all the coasts of dark destruction seek / Deliverance for us all.'

But one cannot have much confidence in his ability to find deliverance. Like so many of the speakers in Ashbery poems his identity is uncertain, lost in the diversity of voices and experiences of which he is constituted. In this respect Daffy is a Satanic or fallen version of the true mode of deliverance, which is indeed to abandon the limits imposed by a closed notion of identity, but by surrendering to the life around us. This, however, is a manoeuvre which requires the circumvention of conventional modes of understanding. The 'background' left out of the film's conventional construction is really a source of new life. Only to the dead is it death. We need the courage to understand and appropriate it. As Ashbery says in 'Self-Portrait in a Convex Mirror':

> It may be that another life is stored there
> In recesses no one knew of; that it,
> Not we, are the change; that we are in fact it
> If we could get back to it.

This is a possibility that also suggests the erosion of boundaries between the objective and the subjective. Ashbery speaks in 'Forties Flick' of 'The indoors with the outside becoming part of you'. His poetry itself is evidence of what can happen when this familiar distinction begins to disappear. In the first place, the subject of an Ashbery poem is compounded of conventions. There is no autonomous individual in Ashbery. Secondly, the struggle to live authentically must be a matter of new experiences generating new conventions. But these will always be, perforce, a revision of old conventions.

Whatever people think postmodernism is or should be, the subject of the erosion of the difference between 'inside' and 'outside' is in fact part of it. One of the most pressing questions in Pynchon's *Gravity's Rainbow* is asked by Pointsman, considering the coincidence of the targeting of rocket attacks in London, late in the war, with the location of Lieutenant Slothrop's love-trysts: 'Could Outside and Inside be part of the same field?'[7] And for Ed Dorn, the most original and adventurous of the younger writers to emerge from Olson's shadow, 'The inside real / and the outsidereal' form a continuum.[8] The punning play on 'sidereal', evoking a cosmos which generates but does not overmaster the imagination, is typical of Dorn, and helps to distinguish him from Olson, who does not cherish such effects. Indeed, the idea of distinguishing himself from Olson makes the occasional appearance in his work. In 'From Gloucester Out', thinking of the master who had written a primer for him, and of the master's town, Dorn refers to 'the guilt / that kills me / My adulterated presence'.[9] Adulterated, perhaps, compared with the purity of Olson's project? Dorn, hailing from the West, was not conscious of the same historical rootedness as he felt in Olson. Yet this is one of the founding conditions of his imaginative freedom, a freedom which permits him to maintain bluntly that 'the art of poetry is not the same thing as, the art of perception.'[10] This is a theme which is gaining currency even among some 'anti-Establishment' poets in Britain. Iain Sinclair, author of the novel *White Chappell*, which won the Guardian Fiction Prize in 1987, has written a long work in prose and poetry, *Lud Heat*, which owes something to Dorn's sense that Olsonian geography can be removed from its objectivist bearings and treated with imaginative freedom. Sinclair makes the sites of the Hawksmoor churches in London, which he convincingly invests with some very sinister associations, the seats of an evil, occult power which operates along the lines of relation between them. As Blake, whom he admires, will take some scientific concept and use it with freedom as a symbol for a mental state, so Sinclair picks up the Olsonian notion of understanding the geography around one and transposes it onto a blatantly imaginative plane. Not that this plane is removed from reference to the objective. As he explains:

> *the objective* is nonsense
> & *the scientific approach* a bitter farce
> unless it is shot through with high occulting
> fear & need & awe of mysteries[11]

Dorn takes a different tack in his long poem *Slinger*, an unabashedly fictional and fantastical poem, which occurs in a semi-imaginary time and place owing something to Westerns and something to the modern movie of paranoia about the corporate society. A character called 'I' meets a 'Cautious Gunslinger' who is seeking Howard Hughes, thought to be in Las Vegas. With a horse called Levi-Strauss, who sits inside the coach and talks philosophy, and with Lil, the 'gaudy madam' of a 'cabaret', they set off on the quest for Hughes. But 'I' is both the first-person pronoun and a character in a third-person narrative:

> The Ego
> is costumed as the road manager
> of the soul, every time
> the soul plays a date in another town
> I goes ahead to set up
> the bleechers, or book the hall
> as they now have it,
> the phenomenon is reported by the phrase
> I got there ahead of myself
> I got there ahead of my I
> is the fact
> which not a few anxious mortals
> misread as intuition . . .
> Yet the sad fact is I is
> part of the thing
> and can never leave it.[12]

Perhaps more interesting than the reference to Heidegger is what the ambiguity about the first-person pronoun does to his narrative. Michael Davidson has put it well: 'The reader becomes caught in a double bind by following a first and third person narration at the same time. Dorn's strategy thus collapses subjective upon objective poles without, at the same time, having to posit a transcendental principle.'[13] This collapse is also a defining characteristic of Ashbery's poetry, though for the more straightforward reason that distinctions between first and third person are often unclear, and in any case, as we have seen, the poems act to make it impossible to establish markers for objective and subjective. Possibly such a collapse will serve the same function for postmodern poetry in general – that having either attacked or lost interest in the problem of discovering a transcendental principle which would guarantee the truth either of the subject or the object, it simply carries on without attempting to fix the position of either pole. This might lead one in theory to expect that myth and even well–shaped narrative (as organizing principles which appeal, however tentatively, to a transcendent reference point) would be treated with a certain ironic levity, and interestingly enough, this is exactly what happens in Ashbery and Dorn. What are the stylistic correlatives of such a view? Certainly, as Marjorie Perloff says, Dorn's poem is 'an ingenious mix of scientific jargon, structuralist terminology, junkie slang, Elizabethan sonneteering, Western dialect, and tough talk'; it also 'accommodates every possible verse form from blank verse and rhymed ballad stanzas to free verse paragraphs and prose interludes.'[14] The same is true of many of Ashbery's poems. The implications of the methods of Joyce, Pound and, not least, Eliot, are again being examined, and without the anxiety about objectivity that afflicts the work of the last two.

If one only had the poetry of Ashbery and Dorn to go on, it would seem easy to agree with Marjorie Perloff that the primacy of the post-Romantic lyric is threatened, and that 'a narrative that is not primarily autobiographical will once again be with us, but it will be a narrative fragmented, dislocated, and often quite literally nonsensical.'[15] But how general is that tendency? A revealing test would be to look at British and Irish poetry. Interestingly enough, one does indeed find a number of poets writing narratives where both what is being narrated and who is doing the narrating are deliberately made mysterious. The work of Blake Morrison and Andrew Motion, including the latter's *Secret Narratives*, is usually regarded with suspicion by the self-appointed guardians of the post-Poundian avant-garde. Certainly in the case of Motion there is a sense of the truth of imagination as it delights in fictions which is hard to distinguish from the position outlined by Sinclair, however different it might sound in its cadences:

> And all of it lies, just as my pictures
> of you at your kitchen table were lies –
> one tender imaginary scene succeeding
> another, but only to prove what is true.
>
> ('The Whole Truth')[16]

But the poet who most obviously approaches the condition outlined by Perloff is Paul Muldoon, in a number of long narrative poems.

The most interesting of these from our point of view is 'Immram', from *Why Brownlee Left*,[17] for its subject-matter, which revolves around the idea of the lost father, itself indicates the absence of a secure originating truth which could guarantee the identity of the narrator. An 'Immram' means a voyage in old Irish, and the poem alludes to the early Irish romance, *Immram Mael Duin*, 'The Voyage of Mael Dun', whose name has an obvious similarity to Muldoon. In the romance the hero's quest is to avenge his father's death. In Muldoon's poem the narrator hunts for his father through various locations in modern California. These locations (pool rooms, 'the Atlantic Club', hotels owned by 'Redpath', whose 'empire / Ran a little more than half way to Hell'), although their boundaries are shifting and uncertain, suggest Chandler, as does the voice of the speaker, and the sense of something complex and corrupt always lying just beyond the scope of detection. The theme of lack of identity announces itself in the first stanza, when the narrator is informed by a fellow pool-player that 'Your old man was an ass-hole. / That makes an ass-hole out of you.' Beneath the crude, but in context rather funny, joke, lies the implication that the narrator is in fact an absence. It is not surprising to find that the identities of other characters are equally uncertain. The narrator meets a girl whose name may be Susan or Suzanne or Susannah. His father, he learns, had fled 'From alias to alias'. Of course, nothing much comes of the quest. His father had been a carrier of contraband:

> But he courted disaster.
> He tried to smuggle a wooden statue
> Through the airport at Lima.
> The Christ of the Andes. The statue was hollow.
> He stumbled. It went and shattered.

Appropriately enough the Logos, or Son, is empty. But we learn nothing more about the father.

There are other ways of escaping the constraints of the poetry of things. Many feminist poets make a conscious virtue of using direct emotive language without any sense that this has to be buttressed by reference to the correct quantity of quasi-symbolic, accurately rendered things. There is a directness, for instance, about many of Adrienne Rich's poems, which goes beyond any debt it might incur to Williams, and is far less cluttered than anything in Plath:

Cruelty is rarely conscious
One slip of the tongue

one exposure
among so many

a thrust in the dark
to see if there's pain there

I never asked you to explain
that act of violence

what dazed me was our ignorance
of our will to hurt each other
('The Photograph of the Unmade Bed')[18]

There are many women poets who cultivate a similar emotional directness.

The use of parodied or fragmented narrative, along with the related
delight in the clash of registers, or, in the case of some feminist poetry,
a lack of embarrassment about the use of directly emotive language
alongside other uses that suggest the special 'object' register of so much
twentieth-century poetry, make it clear that empiricist notions of language as reflection or window or instrument have been replaced by a
conception that could at least inhabit the same universe as the later
Wittgensteinian notion of language-games.[19] Jean-François Lyotard, in
The Postmodern Condition, refers to the 'breaking up of the grand Narratives' in our society.[20] And it could be that it is he who has best
described the connections between the proliferation of new methods of
communication on the one hand, and concepts of the self on the other,
and that his description has relevance to the attempt to describe postmodern poetry:

A *self* does not amount to much, but no self is an island; each exists in a
fabric of relations that is now more complex and mobile than ever before.
Young or old, man or woman, rich or poor, a person is always located at
'nodal points' of specific communication circuits, however tiny these may
be. Or better: one is always located at a post through which various kinds
of messages pass. No one, not even the least privileged among us, is ever
entirely powerless over the messages that traverse and position him at the

post of sender, addressee, or referent. One's mobility in relation to these language game effects (language games, of course, are what this is all about) is tolerable, at least within certain limits.[21]

This is extraordinarily optimistic about 'the least privileged'. And even the more privileged, such as our poets, seem to experience a certain ambivalence, to put it mildly, about the society that has enabled their new freedom of expression. There is Ashbery's open self, discovering new life beyond the constraints of rigid convention. But there is also Daffy Duck, knowingly inhabiting the Hell of a consciousness full of the tawdry detritus of consumerism. There is Muldoon's sheer sense of fun in unfolding his absurd, shape-changing narratives. But there is also the feeling he conveys that the condidion he ascribes to his narrator is bred of powerlessness: that the ability to narrate the old story has been taken away by something in contemporary society, and that this is a loss. Nevertheless, Lyotard's point about communication circuits and language-games, divorced from its optimism about the power people possess in all this, is an illuminating one.

His language-games are scarcely the same entities as Wittgenstein's, being more clearly a matter of different registers in different, specific, technically defined communication circuits. Wittgenstein's, on the other hand, are small-scale fundamentals. Yet clearly the two conceptions are congruent with each other, and the facts they seek to describe may be seen as closely related. Postmodern poetry exists in a world where both concepts of language-game are relevant. The parodies, the absence of embarrassment about using abstract or emotive language, the subversion of narrative expectation – these can be seen as appropriate to a world where extreme self-consciousness about different registers is combined with a rejection of empiricist ideas about language. And there is a sense of the difficulty of attaining some secure vantage point outside and above the games or game. Yet this need not be a pessimistic or frivolous position. Although it appears that writing may be coming to accept the instability of the arc or thread that stretches between uncertain subject and flickering object, it is finding a new playfulness and, paradoxically, confidence there. Such confidence will be strengthened if poets cease to disavow Romanticism in the anxious way that has been such a notable feature of our era. If they do, then male poets may not feel the need to project onto Romanticism that fear of the feminine which goes in part with a crisis of signification: 'My words cannot master the chaotic object or woman. Let me be hard and clear, unlike a woman.' Solitary subject and brute object are being replaced by discourses and their social implications, which seem relatively certain, and have acquired the aspect of opportunity. In the process, poetry may rediscover, in very untraditional combinations and forms, many of the traditional kinds of pleasure that have been denied it in favour of the object.

NOTES

CHAPTER I: THE INHERITANCE: ROMANTICISM AND THE PRESENT DAY

1 Pope, *Imitations of Horace*, Satires, II, vi, 189–96.

2 Anthony Thwaite, *Poetry Today: A Critical Guide to British Poetry 1960– 1984* (London and New York, 1985), pp.109, 110, 115, 116.

3 David Trotter, *The Making of the Reader: Language and Subjectivity in Modern American, English and Irish Poetry* (London and Basingstoke, 1984), p.246.

4 Ted Hughes, *Poetry in the Making* (London, 1976), *passim*; quoted and discussed by Trotter, *Making of the Reader*, p.246.

5 Trotter, *Making of the Reader*, pp.246–9, and see Michael and Peter Benton (eds), *Touchstones 3*, (London, 1969), p.28.

6 John Haffenden, *Viewpoints: Poets in Conversation* (London, 1981), p.182.

7 John Carey, *John Donne: Life, Mind and Art* (London and Boston, 1981), p.151.

8 'Grunts and Groans', *Sunday Times*, 9 December 1979, p.51.

9 Ted Hughes, *Crow* (London, 1970); Geoffrey Hill, *Mercian Hymns* (London, 1971); Seamus Heaney, *North* (London, 1975).

10 Eliot had been influenced by Irving Babbitt's *Rousseau and Romanticism* (Boston and New York, 1919). The dismissive attitude of a generation was summed up in F. L. Lucas's *The Decline and Fall of the Romantic Ideal* (Cambridge, 1936).

11 *Making of the Reader*, pp.70 ff.

12 Edward Lobb, *T. S. Eliot and the Romantic Critical Tradition* (London, Boston and Henley, 1981), p.75.

13 Kingsley Amis, *A Case of Samples: Poems 1946–1956* (London, 1956), pp.30–1.

14 A. J. Ayer, *Language, Truth and Logic*, 2nd rev. edn (London, 1946), p.34. The influence of this work, and of logical positivism, is discussed by Blake Morrison in *The Movement: English Poetry and Fiction of the 1950s* (Oxford, 1980), pp.158–9.

15 A. Alvarez (ed.), *The New Poetry: An Anthology* (Harmondsworth, 1962; revised 1967), p.28.

16 Blake Morrison and Andrew Motion, *The Penguin Book of Contemporary British Poetry* (Harmondsworth, 1982), p.13.

17 *The New Review*, 2, no. 23 (February, 1976), p.37.

18 Tom Paulin, *Liberty Tree* (London and Boston, 1983).

19 Tom Paulin, 'A Naked Emperor?', review of John Ashbery, *A Wave* in *Poetry Review*, 74, no. 3 (September, 1984), p.32.

20 Tom Paulin, *Thomas Hardy: The Poetry of Perception* (London, 1975), p.211.

21 ibid., p.210.

22 ibid., p.45.

23 Geoffrey Thurley, *The Romantic Predicament* (London and Basingstoke, 1983), pp.56–7.

24 ibid., p.43.

25 Isobel Armstrong, *Language as Living Form in Nineteenth Century Poetry* (Brighton and Totowa, N. J., 1982).

26 Frank Lentricchia, *The Gaiety of Language: An Essay on the Radical Poetics of W. B. Yeats and Wallace Stevens* (Berkeley and Los Angeles, 1968), pp.8–20.

27 S. T. Coleridge, *Biographia Literaria*, ed. J. Shawcross, 2 vols (Oxford, 1907), 1, p.100.

28 Lentricchia, *Gaiety of Language*, p.12.

29 Coleridge, *Biographia*, 1, p.185.

30 Friedrich Schelling, *System of Transcendental Idealism* [Sect. VI], trans. Albert Hofstadter, in *German Aesthetic and Literary Criticism: Kant to Hegel*, ed. David Simpson (Cambridge University Press, 1984), p.149.

31 ibid, p.129.

32 Paul Hamilton, *Coleridge's Poetics* (Oxford, 1983), pp.88–9.

33 A. Gerard, 'The Systolic Rhythm: The Structure of Coleridge's Conversation Poems', in *Coleridge: A Collection of Critical Essays*, ed. Kathleen Coburn (Englewood Cliffs, N. J., 1967), pp.78–87.

34 Armstrong, *Language as Living Form*, p.27.

35 Rémy de Gourmont, *Selected Writings*, trans., ed., intro. Glenn S. Burne (Detroit, 1966), pp.11–12.

36 *Coleridge's Shakespearean Criticism*, ed. T. M. Raysor, 2 vols (London, 1930), 2, pp.104–5.

37 *Collected Letters of Samuel Taylor Coleridge*, ed. E. L. Griggs, 6 vols (London,

1956–71), 1, p.626.

38 *The Notebooks of Samuel Taylor Coleridge*, ed. Kathleen Coburn, 3 vols (London, 1957, 1961, 1973), 3, n. 3765.

39 See James C. McCusick, *Coleridge's Philosophy of Language*, Yale Studies in English 195 (New Haven and London, 1986), p.85.

40 *Collected Letters of Coleridge*, 1, p.625.

41 Coleridge, *Treatise on Method*, ed. Alice D. Snyder (London,1934), p.81.

42 Geoffrey Hartman, *Beyond Formalism* (New Haven and London, 1970), p.304.

43 William Hazlitt, *Complete Works*, ed. P. P. Howe, 21 vols (1930–4), 4, p.113.

44 A. D. Moody, 'Telling It Like It's Not: Ted Hughes and Craig Raine', *The Yearbook of English Studies*, 17 (1987), p.170.

45 Michael Riffaterre, 'Interpretation and Descriptive Poetry: A Reading of Wordsworth's "Yew Trees"', in *Untying the Text*, ed. Robert Young (Boston, London and Henley-on-Thames, 1981), p.128, reprinted from *New Literary History*, 4, no. 2 (1973).

46 Jacques Lacan, 'The mirror stage as formative of the function of the I as revealed in psychoanalytic experience', in *Ecrits: A Selection*, trans. Alan Sheridan (London, 1977), p.2.

47 ibid., p.196.

48 cf. ibid., p.207.

49 Lacan, 'The agency of the letter in the unconscious or reason since Freud', *Ecrits*, p.154.

50 ibid., p.165.

51 Jacques Lacan, *The Four Fundamental Concepts of Psychoanalysis*, trans. Alan Sheridan (Harmondsworth, 1977), p.102.

52 ibid., pp.100–3.

53 Robert Young, 'The Eye and Progress of his Song: A Lacanian Reading of *The Prelude*', *The Oxford Literary Review*, 3, no. 3 (Spring, 1979), p.83.

54 Lacan, *Ecrits*, p.2.

55 cf. Lacan, *Four Fundamental Concepts*, pp.230–43.

56 Paul de Man, *The Rhetoric of Romanticism* (New York, 1984), p.7.

57 Walter Pater, 'Coleridge', *Appreciations* (London, 1922), p.80.

CHAPTER 2: EZRA POUND

1 Now gathered in 'A Retrospect', *Literary Essays of Ezra Pound*, ed. T. S. Eliot (London and Boston, 1985), pp.3–14.

2 Peter Makin, *Provence and Pound* (Berkeley, Los Angeles and London, 1978), p.30.

3 ibid., p.31.

4   Unless stated otherwise, references are to Ezra Pound, *Collected Shorter Poems*, 2nd edn (London, 1968).
5   ibid., p.33.
6   *Literary Essays*, p.3.
7   Alan Durant, *Ezra Pound: Identity in Crisis* (Brighton, 1981), *passim*, and esp. pp.23–36.
8   *Literary Essays*, p.9.
9   ibid., p.6.
10 ibid., pp.11–12.
11 ibid., p.43.
12 *Literary Essays*, p.48; *Literary Essays*, p.49; Makin, *Provence*, p.31.
13 *Literary Essays*, p.49.
14 Quoted in Ian F. A. Bell, *Critic as Scientist: The Modernist Poetics of Ezra Pound* (London and New York, 1981), pp.28–9.
15 ibid., p.31.
16 ibid.
17 Ernest Fenollosa, *The Chinese Written Character as a Medium for Poetry*, ed. Ezra Pound: in Pound, *Instigations* (New York, 1920), p.377.
18 ibid., p.364.
19 Bell, *Critic as Scientist*, p.170.
20 Ezra Pound, *Pavannes and Divagations* (London, 1960), p.204.
21 Quoted in Makin, *Provence*, p.31.
22 Quoted in Richard Humphreys, 'Demon Pantechnicon Driver: Pound in the London Vortex, 1908–1920', *Pound's Artists: Ezra Pound and the Visual Arts in London, Paris and Italy*, Tate Gallery (London, 1985), p.58.
23 Ezra Pound, 'Affirmations II: Vorticism', in *Ezra Pound and the Visual Arts*, ed. Harriet Zinnes (New York, 1980), pp.7–8.
24 *Literary Essays*, p.49.
25 Fenollosa, *Chinese Written Character*, footnote to p.378.
26 See for instance Andrew Crozier's comments on British poetry, discussed below in chapter 6.
27 Laszlo K. Géfin, *Ideogram: Modern American Poetry* (Milton Keynes, 1982), p.21.
28 Ezra Pound, 'Vorticism', in Zinnes, *Pound and the Visual Arts*, p.205.
29 cf. Stan Smith, *Inviolable Voice: History and Twentieth-Century Poetry* (Dublin and New Jersey, 1982), p.116.
30 Ezra Pound, *The Cantos* (London, 1975), p.13.
31 cf. Leon Surette, *A Light from Eleusis* (Oxford, 1979), pp.40–1.
32 Ezra Pound, 'Vorticism', *Fortnightly Review*, 96 (1914). Reprint in *Ezra Pound*, ed. J. P. Sullivan, Penguin Critical Anthology (Harmondsworth,

1970), pp.52, 57.

33 'Religio', *Pavannes and Divagations*, p.96.

34 Fenollosa, *Chinese Written Character*, p.382.

35 ibid., p.377.

36 *Literary Essays*, p.21.

37 *Cantos*, p.281.

38 Maud Ellmann, 'Floating the Pound: the Circulation of the Subject of *The Cantos*', *Oxford Literary Review*, 3, no. 3 (Spring, 1979), p.20.

39 Sigmund Freud, 'On Transformations of Instinct as Exemplified in Anal Erotism' (1917) in *The Complete Psychological Works*, trans. J. Strachey (London, 1953–), XIV, p.128.

40 Jacques Lacan, *The Four Fundamental Concepts of Psychoanalysis*, trans. Alan Sheridan (Harmondsworth, 1977), p.184.

41 cf. Ellmann, 'Floating the Pound'.

42 *Literary Essays*, p.21.

43 Marjorie Perloff, *The Dance of the Intellect: Studies in the Poetry of the Pound Tradition* (Cambridge, 1985), pp.12–13.

44 *Cantos*, p.237.

45 *The Letters of Ezra Pound: 1907–1941*, ed. D. D. Paige (London, 1951), p.328.

46 Ezra Pound, *Guide to Kulchur* (New York, 1970), p.65.

47 *Literary Essays*, p.25.

48 ibid., p.283.

49 Antony Easthope, *Poetry as Discourse* (London and New York, 1983), p.158.

50 Basil Bunting, 'On the Fly-Leaf of Pound's Cantos', *Collected Poems* (Oxford, 1978), p.110.

51 *Literary Essays*, p.218.

CHAPTER 3: T. S. ELIOT

1. T. S. Eliot, *Selected Essays 1917–1932* (London, 1932), p.145.

2 ibid.

3 ibid., p.146.

4 ibid., p.18.

5 ibid., pp.18, 19.

6 Remy de Gourmont, *Selected Writings*, trans., ed., intro. Glenn S. Burne (Detroit, 1966), p.114.

7   ibid., p.119.

8   ibid., p.123.

9   *Selected Essays*, p.145.

10   ibid., p.144.

11   cf. Michael Edwards, *Eliot/Language* (Breakish, Isle of Skye, 1975).

12   Hugh Kenner, *The Invisible Poet: T. S. Eliot* (London and New York, 1960), pp.120–2.

13   *Selected Essays*, pp.72, 131–2.

14   ibid., p.71.

15   Donald Davie, 'Pound and Eliot: a distinction', in *Eliot in Perspective: A Symposium*, ed. Graham Martin in (London and Basingstoke, 1970), pp.62–82.

16   T. S. Eliot, *The Waste Land: A Facsimile and Transcript of the Original Drafts Including the Annotations of Ezra Pound*, ed. Valerie Eliot (London, 1971); see also Gertrude Patterson, *T. S. Eliot: Poems in the Making* (London, 1971).

17   See Richard Wollheim, 'Eliot and F. H. Bradley: an account' in Martin (ed.), *Eliot in Perspective*, pp.174–5.

18   Grover Smith, *The Waste Land* (Hemel Hempstead, Winchester Mass., and Sydney, 1983), p.103.

19   Sigmund Freud, *On Sexuality*, ed. Angela Richards, *The Pelican Freud Library*, 7, trans., ed., James Strachey (Harmondsworth, 1977), pp.227–42.

20   Sigmund Freud, *The Interpretation of Dreams*, rev. Angela Richards, *Pelican Freud Library*, 4, trans., ed., James Strachey, assoc. ed. Alan Tyson (Harmondsworth, 1976), pp.367–8.

21   ibid., p.367.

22   ibid., p.368.

23   Peter Ackroyd, *T. S. Eliot* (London, 1985), p.91.

24   Wollheim, 'Eliot and F. H. Bradley', p.173.

CHAPTER 4: WILLIAM CARLOS WILLIAMS

1   Yvor Winters, 'Conclusions', *Forms of Discovery* (1967). Reprinted in *William Carlos Williams*, ed. Charles Tomlinson (Harmondsworth, 1972), p.381.

2   cf. Paul Merchant, *The Epic* (London, 1971), p.90.

3   *The Collected Poems of William Carlos Williams*, 1, 1909–1931, ed. A. Walton Litz and Christopher MacGowan (Manchester, 1987), p.224.

4   William Carlos Williams, *Paterson* (London, 1964), p.11.
5   ibid., pp.39, 34.
6   William Carlos Williams, *Kora in Hell* (San Francisco, 1957), VI, p.24.
7   ibid., XVIII, pp.59–60.
8   ibid., pp.77–8.
9   ibid., p.78.
10 ibid., p.82.
11 Williams, *Collected Poems*, pp.234–5.
12 Williams, *Paterson*, p.34.
13 ibid., p.140.
14 William Carlos Williams, *I Wanted to Write a Poem* (New York, 1978), p.37.
15 Hugh Kenner, *A Homemade World: The American Modernist Writers* (London, 1977), p.65.
16 A. D. Moody, 'Telling It Like It's Not: Ted Hughes and Craig Raine', *The Yearbook of English Studies*, 17 (1987), pp.170–1.
17 Ruth Grogan, 'The Influence of Painting on William Carlos Williams', Tomlinson (ed.), *William Carlos Williams*, p.279.
18 Williams, *Collected Poems*, 1, p.188.
19 ibid., p.192.
20 Williams, *Paterson*, p.52.
21 Williams, *Collected Poems*, p.188.
22 Williams, *Paterson*, p.135.
23 ibid., p.194.
24 ibid., p.65.
25 William Carlos Williams, 'Measure', *Cambridge Opinion*, 41 (Oct. 1965), p.13.
26 William Carlos Williams, *Selected Letters*, ed. John C. Thirlwall (New York, 1957), p.331.
27 ibid.
28 Quoted in Mike Weaver, *William Carlos Williams: The American Background* (Cambridge, 1971), p.82.
29 William Carlos Williams, 'Author's Introduction to *The Wedge*' (1944). Reprinted in Tomlinson (ed.), *William Carlos Williams*, p.141.
30 Weaver, *William Carlos Williams*, p.65.
31 Williams, *I Wanted to Write a Poem*, p.82.
32 Tomlinson (ed.), *William Carlos Williams*, pp.313–14.
33 William Carlos Williams, 'America, Whitman, and the Art of Poetry', *The Poetry Journal*, 8, no. 1 (November, 1917), pp.28, 29.
34 Williams, *Collected Poems*, p.213.

35   ibid., pp.226 – 7.
36   Williams, *I Wanted to Write a Poem*, pp.80 – 2. The passage may be found in *Paterson*, p.96.
37   Jonathan Culler, *Structuralist Poetics* (London, 1975), pp.175 – 6.
38   Williams, *Paterson*, p.15.
39   W. C. Williams, 'Correspondence: The Great Sex Spiral', *The Egoist*, 4, no. 7 (August, 1917), p.111.
40   Williams, *Paterson*, p.11.
41   ibid., p.17.
42   Williams, 'Correspondence', p.111.
43   Williams, *Paterson*, p.24.
44   ibid., p.52.
45   ibid., p.57.

CHAPTER 5: THE AMERICAN THING

1   References are to Marianne Moore, *The Complete Poems* (London, 1958).
2   Charles Olson, *Selected Writings*, ed. Robert Creeley (New York, 1966), p.16.
3   ibid.
4   ibid.
5   ibid., pp.16 – 17.
6   ibid., p.22.
7   ibid., p.113.
8   ibid., p.110.
9   Charles Olson, *Letters for Origin, 1950 – 1956*, ed. A. Glover (London, 1969), pp.57, 58.
10   Charles Olson, *In Cold Hell in Thicket* (New York, 1960), p.35.
11   Joseph Riddel, 'Decentering the Image: The "Project" of "American" Poetics?', in *Textual Strategies: Perspectives in Post-Structuralist Criticism*, ed. J. V. Harari (Ithaca, N. Y., 1979), pp.326, 327, 349 – 50.
12   Charles Olson, *The Maximus Poems* (New York, 1960), p.35.
13   ibid., p.154.
14   Olson, *Selected Writings*, p.24.
15   Olson, *Maximus*, p.13.
16   ibid., p.132.
17   ibid., p.11.
18   Charles Olson, *A Bibliography on America for Ed Dorn* (San Francisco, 1964), pp.11, 13.

19   cf. Charles Olson, *The Special View of History* (Berkeley, 1970), p.41.
20   Olson, *Selected Writings*, p.112.
21   Charles Olson, *Poetry and Truth: The Beloit Lectures and Poems*, ed. G. Butterick (San Francisco, 1971), p.58.
22   Charles Olson, *Call Me Ishmael: A Study of Melville* (London, 1967), pp.57–8.
23   ibid., p.55.
24   Herman Melville, *Moby-Dick*, ed. Harold Beaver (Harmondsworth, 1972), p.241.
25   ibid., p.290.
26   Paul Christensen, *Charles Olson: Call Him Ishmael* (Austin and London, 1975), pp.84–7.
27   Olson, *Maximus*, pp.72–3.
28   Louis Zukofsky, *Prepositions* (London, 1967), p.15.
29   ibid., p.22.
30   ibid., p.25.
31   Quoted in L. S. Dembo, 'Louis Zukofsky: Objectivist Poetics and the Quest for Form', in *Louis Zukofsky: Man and Poet*, ed. Carroll F. Terrell (Orono, Maine, n.d.), p.283.
32   Zukofsky, *Prepositions*, p.18.
33   Louis Zukofsky, *Catullus* (London and New York, 1969).
34   Zukofsky, *Prepositions*, p.15.
35   Louis Zukofsky, *A* (Berkeley, Los Angeles and London, 1978). (Written 1928–74.)
36   ibid., p.563.
37   W. B. Yeats, *A Vision*, reprint of 2nd or 1937 version (London, 1966), pp.4–5.
38   Paul Smith, *Pound Revised* (London and Canberra, 1983), p.139.
39   Zukofsky, *A*, p.127.
40   George Oppen, *Collected Poems* (New York, 1979), p.149.
41   ibid., p.19.
42   ibid., p.182.
43   ibid., p.71.
44   ibid., p.4.

CHAPTER 6: CHARLES TOMLINSON

1   Charles Tomlinson, *The Necklace* (London, 1966), pp.xiv–xv.
2   ibid., p.xv.

3 Charles Tomlinson, 'The Middlebrow Muse', *Essays in Criticism*, 7, no. 2 (April, 1957), p.215.

4 These and succeeding quotations from Stevens are from Wallace Stevens, *The Collected Poems of Wallace Stevens* (London, 1955).

5 William Carlos Williams, *Selected Poems*, ed. Charles Tomlinson (Harmondsworth, 1976), pp.18–19.

6 Charles Tomlinson, *The Way of a World* (London, 1969).

7 *The Collected Poems of William Carlos Williams*, 1, 1909–1931, ed. A Walton Litz and Christopher MacGowan (Manchester. 1987), p.294.

8 Charles Tomlinson, *Seeing is Believing* (London, 1969).

9 Andrew Crozier, 'Thrills and Frills: Poetry as Figures of Empirical Lyricism', in *Society and Literature 1945–1970*, ed. Alan Sinfield (London, 1983), p.231.

10 John Haffenden, *Viewpoints: Poets in Conversation* (London, 1981), p.184.

11 Quoted in Jonathan Wordsworth, Michael C. Jaye and Robert Woof, *William Wordsworth and the Age of English Romanticism* (New Brunswick and London, 1987), p.106.

12 ibid., and see illustrations pp.106–7.

13 Charles Tomlinson, Illustration 6, 'Cloud Head', *Agenda*, 9, nos 2–3 (1971).

14 Calvin Bedient, *Eight Contemporary Poets* (London, 1974), p.5.

15 Charles Tomlinson, *Some Americans: A Personal Record* (Berkeley, Los Angeles and London, 1981), p.13.

16 ibid., pp.14, 33.

17 Jonathan Raban, *The Society of the Poem* (London, 1971), p.161.

CHAPTER 7: TED HUGHES

1 Ted Hughes, *The Hawk in the Rain* (London, 1957).

2 Ted Hughes, *Lupercal* (London, 1960).

3 Martin Dodsworth, 'Ted Hughes and Geoffrey Hill: An Antithesis', *The New Pelican Guide to English Literature*, 8, *The Present*, ed. Boris Ford (Harmondsworth, 1983), p.287.

4 Ted Hughes, *Crow: From the Life and Songs of the Crow* (London, 1970).

5 Ted Hughes, *Gaudete* (London and Boston, 1977).

6 Keith Sagar, *The Art of Ted Hughes*, 2nd edn (Cambridge, 1978), p.191. See *Gaudete*, p.14.

7 Stuart Hirschberg, *Myth in the Poetry of Ted Hughes* (Portmarnock, Dublin, 1981). See esp.pp.177–210.

8   Sagar, *Art of Ted Hughes*, p.11.
9   Robert Graves, *The White Goddess* (London, 1961), p.448.
10   ibid., pp.448–9.
11   Ted Hughes, *Wodwo* (London, 1967).
12   Alan Bold, *Thom Gunn and Ted Hughes* (Edinburgh, 1976), p.125.
13   Hirschberg, *Myth*, p.155.
14   C. G. Jung, *Alchemical Studies* (*Collected Works*, 13) (Princeton and London, 1968), p.229.
15   Hirschberg, *Myth*, pp.158–9.
16   Ted Hughes, *Cave Birds: An Alchemical Cave Drama*, with illustrations by Leonard Baskin (London and Boston, 1978), p.56.
17   Ted Hughes, *Moortown* (London and Boston, 1979), p.168.
18   Hughes, *Gaudete*, p.24.
19   ibid., p.167.
20   ibid., p.65.
21   ibid., p.51.
22   ibid., p.9.
23   ibid., pp.194, 200.
24   ibid., pp.185–6.
25   Ted Hughes, *Remains of Elmet*, with photographs by Fay Godwin (London and Boston, 1979).
26   Hughes, *Gaudete*, pp.181–2.
27   ibid., p.199.

CHAPTER 8: SYLVIA PLATH

1   All references are to Sylvia Plath, *Collected Poems*, ed. Ted Hughes (London and Boston, 1981).

CHAPTER 9: SEAMUS HEANEY

1   Seamus Heaney, *Death of a Naturalist* (London, 1966).
2   Terence Hawkes. *Metaphor* (London, 1972), p.75.
3   Andrew Crozier, 'Thrills and Frills: Poetry as Figures of Empirical Lyricism', in *Society and Literature 1945–1970*, ed. Alan Sinfield (London, 1983), p.230.
4   Blake Morrison, *Seamus Heaney* (London and New York, 1982), pp.29–30.

5   Seamus Heaney, *Preoccupations: Selected Prose 1968–1978* (London, 1980).
6   Seamus Heaney, *North* (London, 1975).
7   Seamus Heaney, 'Mother Ireland', *The Listener* (7 Dec., 1972), p.790.
8   Heaney, *Preoccupations*, p.88.
9   Seamus Heaney, *Wintering Out* (London 1972).
10   *Sweeney Astray*, trans. Seamus Heaney (London and Boston, 1984).
11   Seamus Heaney, *Station Island* (London and Boston,, 1984).
12   *The Kilpeck Anthology*, ed. Alan Halsey (The Five Seasons Press, 1981).

CHAPTER 10: CRAIG RAINE

1   Craig Raine, *The Onion, Memory* (Oxford, 1978).
2   David Trotter, *The Making of the Reader: Language and Subjectivity in Modern American, English and Irish Poetry 1960–1984* (London and New York, 1985), p.249.
3   John Haffenden, *Viewpoints: Poets in Conversation* (London, 1981), p.184.
4   Craig Raine, *A Martian Sends a Postcard Home* (Oxford, 1979).
5   Quoted in *The Norton Anthology of English Literature*, ed. M. H. Abrams, et al., 2 vols, (London and New York, 1986), p.249.
6   Craig Raine, *Rich* (London and Boston, 1984).

CHAPTER 11: POSTMODERNISM: THE RETURN OF THE SUPPRESSED

1   John Ashbery, *The Tennis Court Oath* (Middletown, Conn., 1962).
2   John Ashbery, *Self-Portrait in a Convex Mirror* (New York, 1975).
3   John Ashbery, *Some Trees* (New Haven, 1956).
4   Jonathan Culler, *Structuralist Poetics* (London, 1975), p.169.
5   Jacques Lacan, *The Four Fundamental Concepts of Psychoanalysis*, trans. Alan Sheridan (Harmondsworth, 1977), pp.88–9.
6   John Ashbery, *Houseboat Days* (New York, 1977).
7   Thomas Pynchon, *Gravity's Rainbow* (London, 1974), p.144.
8   Edward Dorn, *Slinger* (Berkeley, 1975), unpaginated [p.111].
9   Edward Dorn, *Collected Poems*, enlarged edn (San Francisco, 1983), p.87.
10   Quoted by Peter Middleton in 'Dorn', *Poetry Information*, nos 20 & 21 (Winter, 1979–80), p.24.
11   Iain Sinclair, *Lud Heat* (London, 1975), p.89.

12 Dorn, *Slinger* [pp.57 – 8].
13 Quoted in Marjorie Perloff, *The Dance of the Intellect: Studies in the Poetry of the Pound Tradition* (Cambridge, 1985), p.166.
14 ibid., pp.167, 168.
15 ibid., p.168.
16 Andrew Motion, *Dangerous Play: Poems 1976 – 1984* (Harmondsworth, 1985), p.53.
17 Paul Muldoon, *Why Brownlee Left* (London, 1980).
18 Adrienne Rich, *Poems Selected and New: 1950 – 1974* (New York, 1975).
19 Adhering to the view advanced by Henry Staten, in *Wittgenstein and Derrida* (Oxford, 1985), which sees Wittgenstein as deconstructing essentializing notions about language.
20 Jean-François Lyotard, *The Postmodern Condition: A Report on Knowledge*, trans. Geoff Bennington and Brian Massumi, foreword by Fredric Jameson (Manchester, 1986), p.15.
21 ibid.

SELECT BIBLIOGRAPHY

This bibliography is intended to provide an indication of the kind of critical and scholarly writings which helped in the writing of this book, especially those which influenced or are congenial to the critical approach to be found therein. It is not, therefore, limited to books cited in the text; nor does every book cited there appear here.

CHAPTER 1: THE INHERITANCE ROMANTICISM AND THE PRESENT DAY

(a) *Romanticism to the Present*

Armstrong, Isobel, *Language as Living Form in Nineteenth Century Poetry* (Brighton and Totowa, N.J., 1982).

de Man, Paul, *The Rhetoric of Romanticism* (New York, 1984).

Hamilton, Paul, *Coleridge's Poetics* (Oxford, 1983).

Hartman, Geoffrey, *Beyond Formalism* (New Haven and London, 1970).

Kermode, Frank, *Romantic Image* (London, 1957).

Lentricchia, Frank, *The Gaiety of Language: An Essay on the Radical Poetics of W. W. B. Yeats and Wallace Stevens* (Berkeley and Los Angeles, 1968), pp.8–20.

McCusick, James C., *Coleridge's Philosophy of Language*, Yale Studies in English, 195 (New Haven and London, 1986).

Miller, J. Hillis, *The Disappearance of God* (Cambridge, Mass., and London, 1963).

Riffaterre, Michael, 'Interpretation and Descriptive Poetry: A Reading of Wordsworth's "Yew Trees"', in *Untying the Text*, ed. Robert Young (Boston, London and Henley-on-Thames, 1981), pp.103–32.

Thurley, Geoffrey, *The Romantic Predicament* (London and Basingstoke, 1983).

Young, Robert, 'The Eye and Progress of his Song: A Lacanian Reading of *The Prelude*', *The Oxford Literary Review*, 3, no. 3 (Spring, 1979), pp.78–98.

(b) *The Present*

Butterfield, R. W. (Herbie) (ed.), *Modern American Poetry* (London and Totowa, N.J., 1984).

Crozier, Andrew, 'Thrills and Frills: Poetry as Figures of Empirical Lyricism', in *Society and Literature 1945–1979*, ed. Alan Sinfield (London, 1983), pp.199–233.

Géfin, Laszlo K., *Ideogram: Modern American Poetry* (Milton Keynes, 1982).

Haffenden, John, *Viewpoints: Poets in Conversation* (London, 1981).

Kenner, Hugh, *A Homemade World: The American Modernist Writers* (London, 1977).

Morrison, Blake, *The Movement: English Poetry and Fiction of the 1950s* (Oxford, 1980).

Smith, Stan, *Inviolable Voice: History and Twentieth-Century Poetry* (Dublin and New Jersey, 1982).

Trotter, David, *The Making of the Reader: Language and Subjectivity in Modern American, English and Irish Poetry* (London and Basingstoke, 1984).

CHAPTER 2: EZRA POUND

Bell, Ian F. A., *Critic as Scientist: The Modernist Poetics of Ezra Pound* (London and New York, 1981).

Bell, Ian (ed.), *Ezra Pound: Tactics for Reading* (London, 1982).

Davie, Donald, *Ezra Pound: Poet as Sculptor* (London, 1963).

Durant, Alan, *Ezra Pound: Identity in Crisis* (Brighton, 1981).

Ellmann, Maud, 'Floating the Pound: The Circulation of the Subject of *The Cantos*', *Oxford Literary Review*, 3, no. 3 (Spring, 1979), pp.16–27.

Ellmann, Maud, *The Poetics of Impersonality: T. S. Eliot and Ezra Pound* (Brighton and Totowa, N.J., 1987).

Makin, Peter, *Provence and Pound* (Berkeley, Los Angeles and London, 1978).

Perloff, Marjorie, *The Dance of the Intellect: Studies in the Poetry of the Pound Tradition* (Cambridge, 1985).

Rabaté, J-M., *Language, Sexuality and Ideology in Ezra Pound's Cantos* (London and Basingstoke, 1986).

Smith, Paul, *Pound Revised* (London and Canberra, 1983).

CHAPTER 3: T. S. ELIOT

Bergonzi, Bernard, *T. S. Eliot* (London, 1972).
Edwards, Michael, *Eliot / Language* (Breakish, Isle of Skye, 1975).
Ellmann, Maud, *The Poetics of Impersonality: T. S. Eliot and Ezra Pound* (Brighton and Totowa, N.J., 1987).
Kenner, Hugh, *The Invisible Poet: T. S. Eliot* (London, 1965).
Lobb, Edward, *T. S. Eliot and the Romantic Critical Tradition* (London, 1981).
Martin, Graham (ed.), *Eliot in Perspective: A Symposium* (London, 1970).
Patterson, Gertrude, *T. S. Eliot: Poems in the Making* (London, 1971).
Pinkney, Tony, *Women in the Poetry of T. S. Eliot: A Psychoanalytic Approach* (London and Basingstoke, 1984).

CHAPTER 4: WILLIAM CARLOS WILLIAMS

Cushman, Stephen, *William Carlos Williams and the Meanings of Measure* (New Haven and London, 1985).
Perloff, Marjorie, 'To Give a design: Williams and the Visualization of Poetry', *The Dance of the Intellect: Studies in the Poetry of the Pound Tradition* (Cambridge, 1985), pp.88–118.
Riddel, Joseph N., *The Inverted Bell: Modernism and the Counterpoetics of William Carlos Williams* (Baton Rouge, 1974).
Tomlinson, Charles (ed.), *Williams Carlos Williams* (Harmondsworth, 1972).
Weaver, Mike, *William Carlos Williams: The American Background* (Cambridge, 1971).

CHAPTER 5: THE AMERICAN THING

(a) *Marianne Moore*
Edwards, Michael, 'Marianne Moore: "Transcendence Conditional"', in *Modern American Poetry*, ed. R. W. (Herbie) Butterfield (London and Totowa, N.J., 1984), pp.110–26.
Kenner, Hugh, *A Homemade World: The American Modernist Writers* (London, 1977), pp. 91–118.
Stapleton, Laurence, *Marianne Moore: The Poet's Advance* (Princeton, 1978).

(b) *Charles Olson*
Christensen, Paul, *Charles Olson: Call Him Ishmael* (Austin and London, 1975).

Kenner, Hugh, *A Homemade World: The American Modernirt Writers* (London, 1977), pp.176–83.

Riddel, Joseph, 'Decentering the Image: The "Project" of "American" Poetics?', in *Textual Strategies: Perspectives in Post-Structuralist Criticism* ed. J. V. Harari (Ithaca, N.Y., 1979).

(c) *Louis Zukofsky*

Kenner, Hugh, *A Homemade World: The American Modernist Writers* (London, 1977), pp.164–8, 187–93.

Smith, Paul, *Pound Revised*, (London and Canberra, 1983), pp.133–54.

Terrell, Carroll F. (ed.), *Louis Zukofsky: Man and Poet* (Orono, Maine, n.d.).

(d) *George Oppen*

Crozier, Andrew, 'Inaugural and Valedictory: The Early Poetry of George Oppen', in *Modern American Poetry*, ed. R. W. (Herbie) Butterfield (London and Totowa, N.J., 1984), pp.142–57.

Hatlen, B. (ed.), *George Oppen: Man and Poet* (Orono, Maine, 1981).

Kenner, Hugh, *A Homemade World: The American Modernist Writers* (London, 1977), pp.168–71, 185–7.

Perloff, Marjorie, 'The Shape of the Lines: Oppen and the Metric of Difference', *The Dance of the Intellect: Studies in the Poetry of the Pound Tradition* (Cambridge, 1985), pp. 119–34.

CHAPTER 6: CHARLES TOMLINSON

Bedient, Calvin, *Eight Contemporary Poets* (London, 1974), pp.1–22.

Raban, Jonathan, *The Society of the Poem* (London, 1971) pp.158–64.

Tomlinson, Charles, *Some Americans: A Personal Record* (Berkeley, Los Angeles and London, 1981).

CHAPTER 7: TED HUGHES

Bedient, Calvin, *Eight Contemporary Poets* (London, 1974), pp. 95–118.

Bold, Alan, *Thom Gunn and Ted Hughes* (Edinburgh, 1976).

Dodsworth, Martin, 'Ted Hughes and Geoffrey Hill: An Antithesis', in *The New Pelican Guide to English Literature*, 8, *The Present*, ed. Boris Ford (Harmondsworth, 1983).

Hirschberg, Stuart, *Myth in the Poetry of Ted Hughes* (Portmarnock, Dublin, 1981).
Sagar, Keith, *The Art of Ted Hughes*, 2nd edn (Cambridge, 1978).

CHAPTER 8: SYLVIA PLATH

Bassnett, Susan, *Sylvia Plath* (Basingstoke, 1987).
Newman, Charles (ed.), *The Art of Sylvia Plath: A Symposium* (Bloomington and London, 1971).
Lane, Gary (ed.), *Sylvia Plath: New Views on the Poetry* (Baltimore and London, 1979).

CHAPTER 9: SEAMUS HEANEY

Corcoran, Neil, 'Seamus Heaney and the Art of the Exemplary', *The Yearbook of English Studies*, 17 (1987), pp.117–27.
Crozier, Andrew, 'Thrills and Frills: Poetry as Figures of Empirical Lyricism', in *Society and Literature 1945–1979*, ed. Alan Sinfield (London, 1983), pp.199–233.
Haffenden, John, 'Seamus Heaney and the Feminine Sensibility', *The Yearbook of English Studies*, 17 (1987), pp.89–116.
Heaney, Seamus, *Preoccupations: Selected Prose 1968–1978* (London, 1980).
Morrison, Blake, *Seamus Heaney* (London and New York, 1982).

CHAPTER 10: CRAIG RAINE

Trotter, David, *The Making of the Reader: Language and Subjectivity in Modern American, English and Irish Poetry* (London and Basingstoke, 1984), pp.248–9.

CHAPTER 11: POSTMODERNISM: THE RETURN OF THE SUPPRESSED

(a) *John Ashbery*
Lehman, David (ed.), *Beyond Amazement: New Essays on John Ashbery* (Ithaca and London, 1980).

Mottram, Eric, 'John Ashbery: "All, in the Refined, Assimilable State"', *Poetry Information*, nos. 20 and 21 (Winter, 1979–80) pp.31–48.

Perloff, Marjorie, '"Transparent Selves": The Poetry of John Ashbery and Frank O'Hara', *The Yearbook of English Studies*, 8 (1978), pp.171–96.

Shapiro, David, *John Ashbery: An Introduction to the Poetry* (New York, 1979).

(b) *Ed Dorn*

Middleton, Peter, 'From Geography to Gunslinger: The Poetry of Edward Dorn', *Poetry Information*, nos. 20 and 21 (Winter, 1979–80), pp.18–30.

Perloff, Marjorie 'Postmodernism and the Impasse of Lyric', *The Dance of the Intellect: Studies in the Poetry of the Pound Tradition* (Cambridge, 1985), pp.172–200.

Wesling, Donald (ed.), *Internal Resistances: The Poetry of Ed Dorn* (Berkeley, 1985).

(c) *Paul Muldoon*

Morrison, Blake, 'The Filial Art: A Reading of Contemporary British Poetry', *The Yearbook of English Studies*, 17 (1987), pp.196–201.

(e) *On postmodernism*

Lyotard, Jean-Francois, *The Postmodern Condition: A Report on Knowledge*, trans. Geoff Bennington and Brian Massumi, foreword by Fredric Jameson (Manchester, 1986).

Perloff, Marjorie, 'Postmodernism and the Impasse of Lyric', *The Dance of the Intellect: Studies in the Poetry of the Pound Tradition* (Cambridge, 1985), pp.172–200.

Index